Garden History: A Very Short Introduction

'As informative as it is accessible, this compact and expertly researched historical chronicle surprises and delights.'

Garden Design Journal

VERY SHORT INTRODUCTIONS are for anyone wanting a stimulating and accessible way into a new subject. They are written by experts, and have been translated into more than 45 different languages.

The series began in 1995, and now covers a wide variety of topics in every discipline. The VSI library currently contains over 550 volumes—a Very Short Introduction to everything from Psychology and Philosophy of Science to American History and Relativity—and continues to grow in every subject area.

Very Short Introductions available now:

WORK Stephen Fineman
WORLD MUSIC Philip Bohlman
THE WORLD TRADE
  ORGANIZATION Amrita Narlikar

WORLD WAR II Gerhard L. Weinberg
WRITING AND SCRIPT
  Andrew Robinson
ZIONISM Michael Stanislawski

Available soon:

FILM NOIR James Naremore
REPTILES T. S. Kemp
CONCENTRATION CAMPS Dan Stone

MATTER Geoff Cottrell
HOMER Barbara Graziosi

For more information visit our website

www.oup.com/vsi/

Gordon Campbell

GARDEN HISTORY

A Very Short Introduction

OXFORD
UNIVERSITY PRESS

OXFORD
UNIVERSITY PRESS

Great Clarendon Street, Oxford, OX2 6DP,
United Kingdom

Oxford University Press is a department of the University of Oxford.
It furthers the University's objective of excellence in research, scholarship,
and education by publishing worldwide. Oxford is a registered trade mark of
Oxford University Press in the UK and in certain other countries

First published in hardback as *A Short History of Gardens* 2016
First published as a Very Short Introduction 2019

Impression: 1

Published in the United States of America by Oxford University Press
198 Madison Avenue, New York, NY 10016, United States of America

British Library Cataloguing in Publication Data

Data available

Library of Congress Control Number: 2018957110

ISBN 978-0-19-968987-3

Printed in Great Britain by
Ashford Colour Press Ltd, Gosport, Hampshire

Contents

Acknowledgements

My principal debt is to my wife Mary, a nurseryman's daughter and trained horticulturalist who has joined me on countless visits to gardens, has taken some of the photographs in this volume, and read an early draft of this book with great care. I have also benefited from the assistance of Thomas Corns, Ebo Aebischer-Crettol, Stella Fletcher, Vicky Lewis, and Hiroko Sano, who have variously read early drafts of chapters or elucidated linguistic points or talked through issues with me. Sheri Repucci kindly corrected my account of Calvert Vaux.

OUP organizes the creation of books in a congenial pass-the-parcel system. Andrea Keegan commissioned the book and Sophie Goldsworthy signed the contract on behalf of the Press. Andrea and Jenny Nugee then carried the book from contract to submission, in the process reading preliminary drafts and soliciting the views of four immensely helpful external readers, two of whom kindly read the completed manuscript. Carrie Hickman was the picture researcher, Dan Harding the copy-editor, Chandrakala Chandrasekaran the production manager, Alannah Santra the in-house production editor, and Alex Walker the cover designer. The proofreader was Dorothy McCarthy, and the index was prepared by Kim Birchall. Marketing was the responsibility of Phil Henderson and Elle Chilvers, and press and publicity were the responsibility of Anna Gell. They constitute a wonderfully supportive team, and I am grateful to all of them.

List of illustrations

Introduction

What is a garden? The term is generally understood to denote a planned outdoor space distinguished from its surroundings by either a formal enclosure or a marked stylistic difference. The contents of a garden are typically partly constructed and partly natural. The design of the garden reflects its purposes, which may be recreational, aesthetic, practical, or contemplative. It is difficult to be more precise, because different cultures have different senses of what constitutes a garden. In the West, for example, gardens are usually centred on horticulture, whereas in the East, gardens are often centred on stones.

What do gardens mean? The cultivation of gardens, which is a joy to many and a tiresome task to others, often stands as a metaphor for the imposition of order: the eloquent gardeners in Shakespeare's *Richard II* compare gardening to the governance of a kingdom, and on a smaller scale, the notion of cultivating one's own garden, which derives from Voltaire's *Candide* ('Il faut cultiver notre jardin'), has the sense of attending to one's own affairs. The notion that our relationship to gardens has a significance beyond the horticultural has long been asserted, hence, for example, the garden plaques that cite Dorothy Frances Gurney's 'one is nearer God's heart in a garden | Than anywhere else on earth'. In 2006, David Cooper, who may be the world's first academic philosopher of gardens, published *A Philosophy of Gardens*, in which he explores the reasons why gardens matter so much to so many people, across cultures, and across time. A vegetable garden, for example, provides food that in developed countries could more easily be accessed in a greengrocer's shop or a supermarket, but even those who could afford to buy vegetables choose instead to grow them, a practice that answers the need to nurture and respect life, to have routines that structure and pattern one's own life, and to bolster one's own health by growing healthy food. The urge to create structures and patterns is also realized in the organization of the vegetable garden, and indeed of the ornamental garden. The allotment garden is a good example of the uses of vegetable gardens beyond the production of food: the allotment provides exercise, fresh air, education in the ways of the natural world, and companionship with fellow allotment holders.

Garden visitors respond to both the organization of the garden and the healthy plants that live there. At a deeper level, the garden represents the interdependence of humans and other parts of the natural world. The garden is a space designated for a partnership between human activity and a compliant natural world. The burgeoning of garden centres around the world in recent decades bears witness to the strengthening of that partnership. And for those who would rather stroll in a garden than weed it, the garden becomes a place of respite. This usually takes a wholly secular form in the idea of the garden as a place for quiet reflection, but Mrs Gurney's notion that a walk in the garden can bring one closer to God is not quite dead, as evidenced in the success of the Quiet Garden Movement, which was founded by an Anglican priest in 1992 with a view to providing still spaces for reflection, prayer, and spiritual renewal; there are now some 300 Quiet Gardens in eighteen countries. Meditative gardens can of course also be secular, as in gardens of remembrance and peace gardens.

The garden is an art form that interacts with nature, as memorably articulated by Polixenes in Shakespeare's *The Winter's Tale*: 'this is an art | Which does mend nature, change it rather, but | The art itself is nature'. This little book is a history of that art. The contours of garden history as a discipline are not well defined, in part because most of the expertise lies outside the universities. Just as in industrial archaeology, where a question about how a Victorian engine works can better be answered by a man in greasy overalls who has spent countless weekends working on Victorian engines than by a professor, so the custodians of the knowledge of garden history are more likely to be impassioned and dauntingly well-informed amateurs rather than academic professionals. This means that the history of gardens tends to be isolated from historically informed discussions of their societal contexts, because the writer's eye is sharply focused on the garden. In recent decades a handful of academic historians, such as Michel Baridon, John Dixon Hunt, Timothy Mowl, and Simon Schama, has striven to redress this imbalance, and while such historians are joining the amateurs who have long been immersed in archives, landscape archaeologists are excavating gardens: some 500 gardens have been excavated at Pompeii and Herculaneum.

The reconstruction of many historical gardens has been based on knowledge produced in archives and in archaeological investigations. The treatment of such knowledge in the reconstruction of gardens is a matter of considerable debate. At Kenilworth Castle, Het Loo, and Mount Vernon there have been attempts to recreate the gardens of a specific year (1575, 1684, and 1799); at Colonial Williamsburg, the archaeology has served as a springboard for modern designs; at Villa d'Este in Tivoli, there has been no attempt to restore the original garden, but some original features have been restored, and sit alongside the innovations of later periods. In earlier periods there were few such scruples: designers of landscape gardens were often content to obliterate earlier gardens.

Our perception of any particular garden is filtered through our cultural memories and our personal experience of gardens. The cultural memory of garden visitors in the Abrahamic tradition goes back as far as the Garden of Eden, which has been endlessly recreated in painting and in gardens. In the Shinto tradition of Japan, the cultural memory extends back beyond the arrival of Daoist and Buddhist mythologies to a time when gods were associated with particular features in the landscape, such as a large boulder or a waterfall, and that memory colours the perception of Japanese gardens. This short book is on one level an overview and a whirlwind survey, but it is also an attempt to set gardens in the context of cultural memory.

My professional duties have occasioned visits to more than seventy countries (on every continent), and in snatches of free time I have been able to visit many gardens. Some have been grand gardens, but others have been modest English gardens far from England, including the hill stations of India and the sites of former BP oil refineries in Iran; such gardens were once an assertion of Englishness, and are now part of the cultural memory of India and Iran.

In this book I try to choose as examples, gardens that I have visited, as feet on the ground are one way of ensuring accuracy. One consequence of this principle is that there is a bias towards substantial gardens that are open to the public. As my subject has a pronounced historical dimension, I must of necessity discuss gardens that no longer exist, but I have nonetheless endeavoured to choose as many examples as possible from gardens that still exist and can be visited. I am conscious that gardens are living creations that never stand still, and at times seem closer to performance art than to art whose form is fixed. That protean quality, which means that knowledge of a garden can quickly be rendered out of date, is nonetheless one of the joys of the garden. Plato famously quotes Heraclitus to the effect that one cannot step into the same river twice; the same might be said of gardens.

Chapter 1
The ancient and medieval garden

The Near East and eastern Mediterranean

The earliest documented gardens were in the area known as the Fertile Crescent, which extended from Egypt north-east through the eastern Mediterranean and then south-east to the Persian Gulf. The Garden of Eden is traditionally located in southern Mesopotamia, the eastern end of the Crescent, near the confluence of the Tigris and the Euphrates. The rivers now converge in Shatt al-'Arab, but in antiquity the rivers ran separately into the Persian Gulf through a place that the Sumerians called 'Edin', which has the sense of fertile, arable land.

There was said to have been no rain in Eden before the fall, but the garden was sufficiently watered by its rivers. The lands of the Assyrians lay in northern Mesopotamia, between the Tigris and the Lesser Zab, and there too the rivers and their tributaries could be used for irrigation. The Assyrian King Sennacherib (r. 704–681 BCE) planted a garden laid out around a central axis in Assur, his first capital. When he moved the capital to Nineveh, Sennacherib commissioned new gardens in which plants were placed in long rows to facilitate irrigation. Sennacherib's successors included Ashurbanipal, who built a new palace in Nineveh. The reliefs with which he decorated its walls included one (now in the British Museum) known as the 'Garden Party' (c.640 BCE).

The king and queen are shown relaxing in a garden under a trellis; the garden ornaments include the head of a defeated rival hanging upside down on the second tree from the left (see Figure 1).

The Hanging Gardens of Babylon derive at least in part from a memory of the gardens of Sennacherib and Ashurbanipal at Nineveh. Archaeologists have not been able to identify definitively the site of these gardens, and in the absence of evidence it remains possible that they were purely legendary. If they did exist, they may have been terraced gardens on the bank of the Euphrates, or may have been landscaped levels of the staged tower (ziggurat) known as the Etemenanki, the prototype of the biblical Tower of Babel. Visual images of the gardens of Mesopotamia survive in wall paintings and stone reliefs, and lists of plants have been found in cuneiform texts. The fragmentary picture that emerges from this evidence is of enclosed courtyard gardens with plants in rows and water (a fountain or a pond) at the centre, and of enclosed parks with orchards and game stocked for hunting.

Further east, Pasargadae (now in central Iran, near Persepolis) was the capital of the Achaemenid Empire and the seat of Cyrus the Great (*r.* 559–530 BCE). The palace complex differs from those in Assyria in that the principal buildings were placed at intervals within the enclosed park rather than grouped together beside the park. The garden was divided into four quadrants by irrigation channels, with a fountain at the middle. This design, known as *chahar bagh* ('four gardens') in Persian and thence absorbed into other Islamic languages (e.g. Urdu), was to become immensely influential in Islamic gardens, not least because the riverine garden of eternal paradise described in the Qur'an is recognizably a garden in the *chahar bagh* tradition.

In Egypt the earliest documented gardens derive from the period of the Old Kingdom (*c.*2575–*c.*2150 BCE). These were enclosed gardens laid out around a rectangular pool. A fragmentary wall painting from the Theban tomb of Nebamun (18th Dynasty,

1. 'Garden Party' relief from the North Palace of Ashurbanipal.

7

*c.*1350 BCE) now in the British Museum shows such a garden pool, which is of a size sufficient to accommodate waterfowl and tilapia. Plants include lotus in the pool, papyrus at its edge, and rows of trees and shrubs (date palms, doum palms, sycamore figs, and mandrakes). The size of the pool and the garden varied with the circumstances and standing of the owner, but the design is remarkably constant, as was the notion of a single access point from the house. The surrounding wall afforded privacy and security but, then, as in modern Egyptian gardens, it also formed a bulwark against desert wind and sand. Within the walls, there was no ground cover; plants were irrigated individually, and between the plants there was bare and dry earth.

Greece and Rome

For students of literature, the enduring image of the early Greek garden is contained in the final pages of Homer's *Odyssey*, in which King Laertes is depicted hoeing his vineyard, and Odysseus proves his identity by recalling lessons in horticulture that his father had given to him as a child. This was a palace garden, but its primary purpose was the production of food, and so it accommodated a vineyard, an orchard, and a vegetable patch. The emphasis on growing food continued into the gardens of the classical and Hellenistic periods, which were in suburbs or in the countryside rather than in cities. Prosperous urban homes had courtyards, but there is no evidence of planting. The only gardens within the city were in public spaces such as parks, and in gardens owned by temples. The glory that was Greece did not include constructed recreational gardens, but places where shade and water were to be found were highly valued, and their uses included recreation; the School of Epicurus was famously centred in such a grove, and was commonly referred to as 'the Garden'.

Roman gardens are well-attested in literature, inscriptions, painting, and archaeology. An idealized image of a villa garden, with a huge range of plants simultaneously in fruit and flower, survives in a set of frescoes on all four walls of a windowless underground dining room (*triclinium*) in the villa of Livia Drusilla (58 BCE–29 CE), third wife of the Emperor Augustus, at Prima Porta, just north of Rome. The frescoes, which are now displayed in the Palazzo Massimo (part of the Museo Nazionale Romano), show a large walled garden with decorative trees (e.g. pine, cypress, pine, turkey oak, holly oak), fruit trees (e.g. date palm, quince, pomegranate), and shrubs (e.g. box, myrtle, oleander).

At Pompeii and Herculaneum it is possible to see archaeologically informed reconstructions of Roman villa gardens presented as they were when Vesuvius exploded in 79 CE. These gardens are extensions of the architecture of the house, often using a peristyle (a colonnade within a building surrounding a courtyard) as a framing device. The peristyle derived from Greek architecture, but in Roman houses it encompassed a garden rather than a stone courtyard. There is an excellent example of a reconstructed peristyle garden with fountains and basins at the 1st-century House of the Vettii in Pompeii. The garden was irrigated by its access to an aqueduct, which provided the water for fountain statuettes that emptied into the marble basins, and for the two fountains within the garden. Some of the neighbouring gardens had displays of garden sculpture, and many had a central pool.

Elsewhere in Italy, gardens were sometimes more spacious than those in the shadow of Vesuvius. Hadrian's villa near Tivoli had terraced gardens with a nymphaeum (an architectural grotto with fountains and statues) at one end, still partially standing. The two villas of Pliny the Younger, vividly described in his letters, had topiary and statues. When Romans migrated to the provinces of the empire, they recreated Roman gardens. The finest survivors, both enhanced by a measure of reconstruction, are at Conimbriga (Portugal), which is remarkable for its use of hundreds of jets of water, and Fishbourne (England), where the northern half of the garden has been replanted using the results of archaeological analysis.

South Asia

South Asia has a long and rich cultural history, and early gardens have for the most part been overlaid with later Islamic or Western gardens. The surviving evidence for these ancient gardens is mostly literary and artistic rather than archaeological, so it is difficult to judge the relationship between the ideal gardens of the imagination and the actual gardens laid out in antiquity. Given the heat of South Asia, it is not surprising that the paradise of the early Hindu, Jain, and Buddhist imagination was a cool and well-watered alpine domain centred on Mount Meru, which Buddhists know as Sumeru. The gardens of this sacred domain are chiefly remarkable for the importance of their trees, which have long had a particular significance in Indian culture: there is evidence that the peepal tree was worshipped in the Indus Valley Civilization, and in Hinduism the peepal tree is associated with Vishnu, the bel (wood apple) with Shiva, and the neem with Surya. These and other sacred trees (banyan, mango, ber) were in the gardens of the gods, and so were planted in the grounds of temples.

One of the principal literary sources of the ancient Indian garden is the *Kāmasūtra*, which is not normally consulted for its horticulture. The sensuousness of sexual congress was deemed to be enhanced and complemented by sensual properties of the garden, which offered the cooling shade of trees, the sight and smell of flowers, and the serenity of a pond at the centre of the garden.

The most remarkable survivor of the ancient gardens of the subcontinent is Sigiriya, a Buddhist site in central Sri Lanka (see Figure 2). The site is centred on a vast rock that rises out of the surrounding jungle. The site has been occupied since the 3rd century BCE, but its real importance lies in the decision of King Kasyapa I to locate his court there as a refuge from his enemies.

2. Water gardens at the base of Sigiriya, Sri Lanka.

Kasyapa only lived at Sigiriya for eleven years (484–95 CE), but in that period he created a fortified palace (now a ruin) with large gardens at the western entrance, embellished with canals, fountains, pools, and pavilions. At the lowest level there is a series of three water gardens laid out on an east–west axis; at the foot of the rock there is a group of boulder gardens linked by footpaths. The path upwards leads through terraced gardens to the summit, where there are several unrestored gardens.

In terms of Sri Lankan history, Sigiriya seems to be an isolated survival of an ancient garden. Considered in the broader context of Buddhist cultures, however, it is part of the long history of Buddhist gardens that influence the traditions of China and Japan. Gardens crossed cultural borders centuries before the idea of a national border created artificial boundaries.

The medieval European garden

Our understanding of the medieval European garden is compromised by the fact that none survives in its original form or with its original planting. There is, however, considerable documentation in written texts and visual representations (paintings, tapestry, and manuscript illumination), though it is often difficult to tie this information to known gardens, and the illustrations are skewed towards the end of the period (the 14th and 15th centuries) and towards Flanders. More stable evidence includes artefacts and the knowledge derived from archaeology.

There are of course exceptions to these generalizations: the detailed plan of an ideal monastery (with a cloister and three additional gardens, plus a cemetery garden), preserved in the library of the Benedictine Abbey of St Gall (Switzerland), is early 9th century, and the gardens of the Château de Dourdan are wonderfully illustrated in the *Très Riches Heures du Duc de Berry* (1416). There is another helpful source in Boccaccio's *Decameron* (1348), which describes the walled garden of what may be the Villa Palmieri near Florence. This garden contained arbours, vine pergolas, walks shaded by citrus trees and jasmine, a marble fountain, and a square flower garden with many varieties of flowers—the characteristic features of a medieval garden.

The key feature of the medieval garden is that it was enclosed. The colonnaded peristyle that framed Roman gardens evolved into the cloister of the medieval monastery, and such cloisters contained gardens. The symbolism of enclosure extended to a spiritual meaning, as can be seen from the use of the Latin term *hortus conclusus* ('enclosed garden') to denote both a type of garden and the Virgin Mary. In medieval readings of the Vulgate version of Song of Songs 4:12 (*Hortus conclusus soror mea, sponsa, hortus conclusus, fons signatus*, 'A garden enclosed is my sister, my spouse; a garden enclosed, a fountain sealed up') the enclosed garden was deemed to represent the church as the bride of Christ.

When translated into actual gardens (which were sometimes known as 'Mary gardens'), plants mentioned in the Song of Songs were often grown, and flowers acquired a symbolic significance. The association of the Virgin with the rose meant that many *horti conclusi* were rose gardens, typically laid out in quadrants with a fountain at the centre, and enclosed by a hedge or wall. There were often arbours, raised flower beds, turfed seats and (in the 15th century) topiary, and sometimes there was grass in which flowers were planted, and trellises with climbing roses. Some of these enclosed gardens were ecclesiastical, but those that belonged to the nobility had a secular dimension. They were laden with meaning, but were in practice used for pleasure and respite, and sometimes for entertainment. This may be because the symbolic weight given to plants in literature and visual representations was not carried over, at least with the same force, into real gardens. It is striking, however, that pictorial representations of these gardens always show human activity,

13

which ranges from the contemplative to the raucous and the mildly improper. As such they were usually distinct from the more functional kitchen gardens and physic gardens of the late Middle Ages, though these too had formal properties such as planting in rows.

The finest gardens in medieval Europe were the Islamic gardens of Andalusia; they will be considered in the chapter on Islamic gardens.

Byzantium

The link between the Roman garden and the Islamic garden is to be found in Byzantium and its empire, which at its greatest extent (under Justinian in the 6th century) almost encircled the Mediterranean, and by the time of its collapse in 1453 consisted only of the enclave of Constantinople. No Byzantine garden survives, but their appearance is well documented in visual representations that survived periods of iconoclasm because they had no religious content. One example from $c.400$ CE is a mosaic from Tabarka (on the coast of what is now Tunisia) and now in the Bardo Museum in Tunis (see Figure 3). It shows an early Byzantine villa set in a landscaped park with trees, trained vines, and ornamental birds.

There is also literary evidence in the form of horticultural manuals, and perhaps less reliable evidence in Byzantine romance, where the pleasure garden features prominently, usually as a setting for meetings of trysting couples. At the other end of the spectrum from landscaped parks and gardens of the romantic imagination, there is considerable evidence of gardens for fruit and vegetables near peasant dwellings and monasteries. This is a tradition that proved to have a long afterlife, because Byzantine designs were later to influence the gardens of their Ottoman successors.

3. Floor mosaic depicting a Byzantine villa, from Tabarka (Tunisia), *c.*400 CE (Musée National du Bardo, Tunis).

Central and South America

The medieval period in Europe coincided with the zenith of the pre-Columbian societies of Central and South America. Activity was focused in these areas because the inhabitants of North America did not have urban centres of a sort that were to develop in Mesoamerica and the Andes. Little is known of Mayan gardens, but there is considerable evidence from literary sources of Aztec gardens. By the mid-13th century the Aztec capital of Tenochtitlán (on the site of what is now Mexico City) was surrounded by lakes (Xochimilco and Chalco) on which market gardens on artificial islands (now known as chinampas) were constructed to extend the amount of arable land. These islands, which were typically rectangles up to 100 metres in length and 8 metres in width, were built in shallow water beside the lake shore. The designated area was enclosed with reeds woven through stakes, and then filled with layers of rock and soil and weed from the lake, and built up to a level about half a metre above the surface of the lake. Chinampas supplied both food (beans, squash, chilli, and maize) and flowers (including dahlias and marigolds) to the cities. Some of these chinampas still survive at Xochimilco, the only remnant of the lake-filled landscape of Tenochtitlán, and now cater to tourists as well as city dwellers.

Within Tenochtitlán, as the conquistador Hernán Cortés attested, many houses had gardens, and there were hanging roof gardens on palaces. In the mid-15th century, Motecuhzuma I had created a walled garden with ornamental and medicinal plants; after the Spanish Conquest it became a public park, and the site is now the Bosque de Chapultepec. Motecuhzuma II also had gardens at Iztapalapa (now buried under the Mexico City suburb of the same name), where there were walkways and fountains as well as ornamental planting, and at Huaxtepec, a specimen garden also used for ritual purposes. In Texcoco, to the north-east, the palace gardens of Nezaualcoyotl contained specimen collections gathered from the empire. These gardens were watered by means of an aqueduct originating in a spring in the mountains to the east. The summit of the hill of Texcotzingo, which Nezaualcoyotl fashioned as a shrine for Tlaloc, the Aztec god of rain and fertility, seems to have been laid out in hanging gardens.

There is less evidence of gardens within the Inca Empire. Chan Chan, the capital of the Chimu Empire, which was eventually conquered by the Incas, is the largest adobe city in the Americas, and it seems reasonable to infer that the empty rectangular spaces amid the ruins were gardens. Close to the Inca capital of Cuzco, the Spanish chronicler Garcilaso de la Vega described the royal gardens at Yucay, which were said to be artificially irrigated, and planted with trees and flowers collected from other parts of the empire.

The Aztec and Inca empires were crushed by their European conquerors, and the design of their gardens left no discernible imprint on European gardens. Their plants, however, were immensely influential, because these gardens bequeathed to Europe and the wider world staples such as potatoes and corn, vegetables such as avocados, beans, peppers, tomatoes, and squash, and, after an interval of several centuries, quinoa. This was one side of what historians refer to as the Columbian exchange, which refers to the biological and cultural exchanges between Europe and the Americas in the wake of Columbus's voyages. Gardens and their plants, from this perspective, were early players in the process of globalization that characterizes the modern world.

Chapter 2
The Islamic garden

The origins of the Islamic garden are a subject of considerable debate which centres on the relative importance of two earlier traditions, those of ancient Rome and ancient Persia. The linear axis and peristyle courtyard of the Roman garden, of which the best surviving example is Conimbriga (Portugal), is certainly an important influence. Some argue that it is the only significant influence on the great Islamic gardens of Spain, and resist the notion of Persian influence. Others champion the influence of ancient Persia, where the walled palace garden was a rectangle divided into quadrants by intersecting irrigation channels (with a fountain in the middle). This design, known as *chahar bagh* ('four gardens'), was to find its greatest written expression in the Qur'an, which describes the garden of eternal paradise (*jannat al-Khuld*) as being irrigated by four rivers (of water, wine, milk, and honey) and beautified with a fountain. This model certainly influenced Islamic garden design in the Middle East and the Indian subcontinent, but there is debate about whether it spread as far west as Moorish Spain and Portugal. My view is that its influence can indeed be discerned there. The gardens of the Alhambra, in Granada, embody both traditions: the Patio de los Leones (Court of the Lions) is divided into quadrants (see Figure 4), and the Patio de los Arrayanes (Court of the Myrtles) is linear.

4. Patio de los Leones (Court of the Lions), Alhambra, Granada, Spain.

Islamic gardens were (and are) centred on water, which retains a special place in Islamic cultures, in part because of its scarcity in the Islamic homelands of the Middle East. Pools of water reflect adjacent buildings and, especially in Spain and Portugal, glazed polychrome tiles (*azulejos*, from Arabic *al-zulayj*, 'polished stone') reflect the still surface of the water. There are occasional fountains, always sufficiently understated so that the tranquillity of the garden is not compromised. Complexes of pools are often connected by water channels that run beside paved footpaths. The abundance of the scarce commodity of water in the garden, and the demonstrable fecundity that ensues from its presence, gesture towards the prosperity and comfortable leisure enjoyed by those with sufficient wealth and standing to be able to own such gardens. The well-ordered Islamic garden is a mirror of the abilities and authority of the ruler, reflecting in miniature the governance of the realm.

The traditional Islamic world extends from Morocco and Mauritania in north-west Africa to Indonesia and Mindanao (in the Philippines) in East Asia. The Islamic garden extends as far west as Morocco, but in the east it does not extend beyond the Indian subcontinent, perhaps because water is not a scarce commodity in the rainforests of South East Asia. The account that follows will begin with the Mughal gardens of the Indian subcontinent and move westwards to the gardens of Spain and Portugal.

The Mughal garden

The Mughal Empire brought the traditions of Iran and Central Asia to what is now eastern Afghanistan, Pakistan, Bangladesh, and all but the southernmost part of India. Mughal rule of the subcontinent was established in 1526, prevailed until 1707, and lived on in ever-diminishing form until 1858, when the last of the Mughals was overthrown after the Mutiny and exiled to Burma.

Garden design inevitably changes when it moves to areas with different climate and soils, and when those who commission gardens have distinctive cultural backgrounds and strong personal tastes. Mughal gardens are Islamic, but they have less moving water and more symmetry than their Central Asian predecessors. The Turkic and Mongolian strain in the cultural ancestry of the Mughal emperors is reflected in the tents and carpets to be found in their gardens. The golden age of Mughal gardens extends from the rule of Babur, the first emperor (r. 1526–30), to that of Aurangzeb (r. 1618–58), the sixth emperor. Each of these emperors is associated with important gardens.

Babur's first garden, and the oldest Mughal garden in India, is Ram Bagh, in Agra, a few miles from the Taj Mahal. The garden, on the left bank of the Yamuna (or Jumna), was built in 1528. The design is firmly in the tradition of the Persian *chahar bagh* (in the subcontinent usually written 'charbagh'), and so is divided into four quadrants by intersecting irrigation channels. Babur built a series of gardens along the river, but it is likely that Ram

Bagh is the garden that he described in detail in his memoirs. Elements of the original design still in place include the three terraces through which water descends in narrow watercourses, the well from which the garden was watered, the stone viewing areas (chabutras) at the corners, and some fountains.

The principal building associated with Humayun, the second Mughal emperor, is his tomb in Delhi, which was built by his widow in 1569–70. The tomb, which inaugurated a tradition of Indian garden tombs that was to culminate a century later in the Taj Mahal, is set in a large charbagh garden that was built on a scale that was unprecedented in India. The bisecting water channels give the illusion of passing under the tomb, which reflects the Quranic tradition that the Garden of Paradise was irrigated by rivers flowing beneath it.

The third Mughal emperor was Akbar, during whose reign the Mughal Empire expanded threefold. The greatest garden associated with his reign is near Wah (in the Pakistani sector of the Punjab), on the Grand Trunk Road north-west of Islamabad. Shah Jahan commissioned the reworking of an existing garden in 1639. His architect for the project, Ahmed Maamar Lahoree, laid out the gardens in charbagh style, with walls, canals, paths, and a number of buildings, including steam rooms (hammams). Shah Jahan subsequently visited the gardens on four occasions, and the Emperor Aurangzeb visited in 1676, but thereafter the garden declined. It is now being restored, and when I visited a few years ago, signage described a plan to replant the fruit trees that once filled the garden.

The fourth Mughal emperor was Jahangir, who is associated with two gardens in Kashmir: Shalimir Bagh and Vernag. Shalimir Bagh was commissioned by Jahangir (who used it as his summer residence) and completed by his son Shah Jahan, who extended it to its present size. It lies close to the northern shore of Lake Dal, to which it was connected by a canal. The garden is now reached by road, but was originally accessed by boat along the canal. The traditionally flat charbagh garden had to be modified to accommodate the rolling landscape, so the garden was laid out on three terraces, united by a canal that runs the length of the garden; the landscape enabled the garden to accommodate hundreds of fountains.

Jahangir's other Kashmiri garden is Vernag (also spelt Verinag), south-east of Srinagar. The garden originated in the landscaping of a spring. The water was captured in an octagonal stone basin, around which an arcade was constructed in 1620. Both have been well restored, but the larger garden surrounding this complex, commissioned by Jahangir and Shah Jahan, survives only in fragments. The stone basin is drained by a canal into the Bihat river some 300 yards distant. The transverse canals, the pavilions, the perimeter walls, and many of the trees have disappeared, but the garden is maintained to a good standard, in part because this Islamic garden now serves as a Hindu shrine.

Shah Jahan, the fifth Mughal emperor, is forever linked in the popular imagination with the Taj Mahal, in Agra. Generations of tour guides and besotted commentators have draped a skein of romantic myths around the wondrous building: that it was built as a monument to love, that the architect's hands were amputated (or he was blinded) to prevent him from building anything else, that Shah Jahan spent his final years under house arrest in the Red Fort (then a palace) gazing wistfully across a bend in the Yumana at the monument to his beloved wife, that he planned an identical mosque in black marble on the opposite bank, and so on.

Taking a cool view of these venerable myths does not necessitate demeaning the building. Indeed, the visitor's first glimpse of the building through the entrance gate is overpowering, even if diminished by the industrial smog of Agra. Shah Jahan's third wife, Mumtaz Mahal, died in 1631, and the Taj Mahal was commissioned as her imperial tomb. When the emperor died in 1666, their daughter Jahanara arranged for him to be buried beside the empress; she died first, so she occupies the central space in the tomb.

This was the fourth and finest of the great Mughal garden tombs, after Humayun's tomb in Delhi, Akbar's in Sikandra, and Jahangir's in Lahore. Its three predecessors were all set in the middle of charbagh gardens, but the Taj Mahal breaks with this pattern by situating the tomb on a terrace at the river's edge, at one end of the garden. Excavations in the 1990s of the ruined Mahtab Bagh ('Moonlight Garden') on the opposite bank of the Yamuna revealed not the foundations of an imagined black Taj, but rather a charbagh garden that mirrored in size and shape the garden in front of the Taj Mahal. This garden's large octagonal pool was clearly designed to reflect the Taj. This discovery revealed a new setting for the tomb: it was in a sense set at the edge of a garden, but in the larger setting, it was built at the river boundary between two adjacent gardens, both of which were constructed in a traditional idiom but on an unprecedented scale. The surviving garden in front of the Taj is in significant part an early 20th-century reconstruction based on what was then current scholarship. The area that is now grassed was once planted with fruit trees. The canal that stretches from the entrance gate to the tomb recalls the original design, as does its raised basin.

The greatest garden associated with Aurangzeb, the sixth Mughal emperor, is now officially known as the Yadavinra Gardens (named in honour of a former maharaja) but popularly known as the Pinjore Gardens. This garden, in Haryana (in what was formerly in the Punjab), was built by Nawab Fidai Khan, the foster brother of Aurangzeb. The central canal survives, as do many fountains and some of the original pavilions, but there are now many modern attractions, including a Japanese garden, a plant nursery, picnic gardens, and a small zoo.

Mughal gardens have been appropriated as part of the cultural heritage of the subcontinent, even in Hindu-dominated India. The garden created by Edwin Lutyens for the Viceroy's Residence (now the Presidential Residence, Rashtrapati Bhavan) in New Delhi, for example, is a Mughal design, albeit with some English planting, including a lawn in the centre used for receptions. A walled circular garden is planted with roses enclosed by rose hedges; walking around it, the visitor experiences a moment of Englishness in an Islamic garden in a predominantly Hindu country. It is testament to the rich hybridity of Indian culture.

Central Asia

The Islamic gardens of Central Asia are often called Timurid Gardens, with reference to Timur the Lame, popularly known in the Anglophone world as Tamerlane or (because of Christopher Marlowe's play) Tamburlaine. Timur was a 14th-century Turko-Mongol ruler of a vast empire that extended from Russia to India, and from Turkey to Mongolia; he established his capital at Samarqand, in what is now Uzbekistan. He was a conqueror of legendary brutality, but also a patron of the arts and of architecture, including garden architecture. The gardens that he commissioned were designed to accommodate a perpetually mobile court, and so pitched tents often sat alongside permanent pavilions. A symbolical representation of these tents survives in the form of the Ottoman garden kiosk, of which several can still be seen at the Topkapı Palace in Istanbul; their attenuated descendants include the 'Turkish Tent' in gardens such as Painshill, in Surrey.

No substantial Timurid garden survives. Timur built a palace in central Samarqand, but when not on military campaigns often chose to live at palaces set in pleasure gardens. The only significant vestige of a Timurid garden is Aq Saray, Shakhrisabz (formerly Kesh, in Uzbekistan), which was Timur's birthplace. The garden layout can no longer be discerned, but it is clear that there were garden pavilions faced with blue tiles, and that the interiors were decorated with wall paintings. There is pictorial and literary evidence of many other Timurid gardens, but little remains above ground. The vast Timurid garden north-east of Herat (in what is now Afghanistan), for example, survives only as monumental earthworks. The rich historical evidence provides many details of the gardens beyond the *chahar bagh* design. There were pavilions for recreation, and the plantings included artificial trees, sometimes fashioned from leather and festooned with jewels.

The importance of these gardens for historians is that they are the conduits through which ancient Persian garden design was transmitted to the Indian subcontinent, so giving birth to the Mughal garden. The link was Babur, the Timurid prince who was to found the Mughal Empire.

Iran

The *chahar bagh* design that originated in ancient Persia survived into the Islamic period, but no early gardens survive, and their appearance must be inferred from literary and pictorial sources, including garden carpets as well as manuscript illuminations. These gardens were bounded by walls, along which lines of poplars were planted. The garden's central axis was a canal flanked by paved walkways and planted areas. The focus of the garden was a water tank with a pavilion, from which the viewer could see fruit trees planted in rows, and beds of scented flowers.

Detailed accounts of Persian gardens first arise with reference to Isfahan, in which the royal gardens were laid out after the city became the capital in 1598; thereafter a steady stream of visitors from Persia, the Arab world, and Europe meant that the gardens were often described. This interaction with the wider world also meant that traditional Islamic elements were juxtaposed with

European features, including topiary. Central Isfahan still has the feel of a city built in a royal garden, because part of the structure of the original garden is preserved in Char Bagh Boulevard, a lengthy pedestrian walkway that runs along the course of what was the central promenade, which had a water channel running down the centre. The cypress and plane trees that originally flanked the walkways have gone, as have the basins and fountains and cascades, but the avenue is still bordered by parks and the gardens of grand houses as well as modern shops and apartments.

The Middle East

Early Islamic gardens in the newly conquered territories in the Middle East were of a type known in Arabic as a *hayr*, a substantial enclosed space used by the king and court for hunting and agriculture. The earliest examples, built by the Umayyad caliphs in the early 8th century, are desert palaces. The best known is Khirbat al-Mafjar, a palace in the West Bank near Jericho that was built by the high-living caliph al-Walid II, whose murder was to end the Umayyad Caliphate. The enclosed garden was irrigated by aqueducts to supply the arable land, but the enclosure also seems to have accommodated a game reserve. Garden buildings included a domed pavilion with a nearby fountain.

The transition from the *hayr* to the ancient *chahar bagh* model associated with subsequent Islamic design can be seen in Samarra, the short-lived ancient capital of the Abbasid Caliphate on the east bank of the Tigris north of Baghdad. South of the city there was a huge mid-9th-century *hayr* garden (the Hayr al-Wuhush) used as a zoological park. The garden was irrigated by means of a large canal, one branch of which (according to literary sources) led to a pool close to the palace, decorated with fountains shaped like birds and animals. Nearby there was a small garden in which was placed a man-made mound, perhaps the remote original of the Renaissance mount. Samarra was abandoned within a century of its foundation, but its influence outlived the city. The 10th-century Madinat al-Zahra, on the west side of Córdoba, was built as a conscious imitation of Samarra. The contention that the *chahar bagh* gardens of Samarra were a model for the later gardens of the Maghreb and Islamic Spain remains a subject of scholarly debate.

The Ottoman Empire

The Ottomans were the successors of the Byzantine Empire, so Ottoman gardens reflect a blend of Byzantine and Islamic forms. The Byzantine villa with its landscaped park survives in Ottoman design, as does the Islamic courtyard garden. In the Balkans, the prevailing model of cultural descent involves a denial of Ottoman influence, so the courtyard garden is sometimes described as a national revival form (as at Koprivshtitsa, Bulgaria), but its Islamic origins are readily apparent.

The imperial garden in the Topkapı Palace in Istanbul became the model for palace gardens in the provincial courts of the Ottoman Empire. The first three courtyards of the Topkapı were planted like walled parks, often with cypress. These areas were sometimes used as a zoological park for animals such as gazelles. Only the fourth courtyard, beyond the harem, had flowerbeds, but in the 17th century the land was increasingly taken over by marble kiosks, of which the first two were garden rooms (with fireplaces), and the third a place from which to view the Bosphorus Strait. These structures, together with a late 16th-century reflecting pool, eliminated planting space, so a new terrace garden was laid out on the slope below the harem.

Despite the shortage of horticultural space, the palace ordered prodigious quantities of bulbs. In 1579, for example, the sultan ordered 50,000 tulips. It is difficult to know where they were planted, but it seems likely that some were planted indoors. In Western Europe, the association of the tulip with the Sublime Porte occasioned the economic bubble known as 'tulip mania' (centred in the Netherlands in the late 1630s); a century later, the 'tulip period' in the Ottoman Empire (*c.*1718–30) saw the tulip become an emblem of noble taste. The Ottoman tulip had ceased to be a decorative garden plant, and instead became an emblem of conspicuous expenditure.

Spain

The finest gardens of the European Middle Ages were those of Islamic Spain. The Muslim conquerors of Spain and Portugal in the 8th century took possession of buildings and gardens that reflected Roman, Visigothic, and vernacular influences. The Hispano-Islamic gardens that emerged from this blend of cultures often recall the *chahar bagh* tradition in their quadripartite structure, and typically structured space with paved walkways that incorporated water channels leading to a central pool. The planting within these geometrical areas, however, was more loosely structured than in earlier Islamic gardens.

Little is known of the gardens of the Umayyad Caliphate that brought Islam to Spain (and in 969 mutated into the independent Umayyad Caliphate of Córdoba), but the gradual excavation since the early 20th century of Madinat al-Zahra, on the western edge of Córdoba, together with the surviving ruins and literary sources, has enabled scholars to develop an understanding of the principal gardens, which were laid out on a series of terraces on a steep slope. The design reflects the influence of the landscape architecture of Samarra accommodated to local conditions and to a local tradition of estates that provided for agriculture, zoological gardens, and pleasure gardens. Three of the gardens have standing remains and have been excavated. Discoveries include the earliest known instance in an Islamic garden of a building being erected on a platform in a pool.

In 1031 the caliphate of Córdoba collapsed. Its principal successor was the Almohad Caliphate, which established its capital in

Seville, where excavations in the Alcázar have revealed successive layers of Islamic gardens. The earliest garden had sunken flower beds flanking what seems to have been a central water tank; the walls around the sunken beds were painted with Moorish arches. In the garden built over this one in the 12th century, the layout is quadripartite, with four deep beds flanked by blind brick arches, and a pool in the centre; clusters of dwarf orange trees were planted in each corner. Elsewhere in the Alcázar, another early garden had intersecting channels of water on top of arches beneath which visitors walked, with water descending to the plants below.

In 1212 the Almohad Caliphate was defeated in battle by the combined Christian forces driving the Reconquista, and in the ensuing decades the Moorish cities of Córdoba (1236) and Seville (1248) fell to the Christians. Thereafter the last Islamic state in Spain was the Sultanate of Granada, which was ruled by the Nasrid dynasty until its defeat in 1492. The palace and gardens of the Alhambra and the Generalife in Granada are justly famed, though in common with all living gardens, the gardens that huge numbers of visitors now enjoy are the descendants of the original gardens.

The earliest gardens of the Alhambra resemble those at Madinat al-Zahra, in that both had central water tanks, transverse water channels alongside walkways, and an abundance of fountains. In the case of the 11th-century Alhambra, some of the fountains took the form of marble lions from whose mouths water flowed. Three hundred years later, in the 14th century, twelve of these lions were moved to the newly constructed courtyard now known as the Patio de los Leones (Courtyard of the Lions), and there they surround the covered alabaster basin; water from their mouths feeds the channels in the courtyard (see Figure 4).

One notable feature of the Patio de los Leones is that, although it is enclosed, the west wall is pierced and has a projecting *mirador,* which, like its cousins the belvedere and the gazebo, affords a view of the gardens. The abundance of *miradores* throughout the palace complex constitutes a clear departure from the earlier architectural tradition that emphasized privacy. The Patio de los Leones is, in terms of garden history, the most important garden in the palace complex; it is also the most Islamic of Spain's Moorish gardens. The *mirador* idea is new, but older traditions are reflected in other aspects of the courtyard. The quadripartite layout recalls the tradition of the Islamic garden, and the columned arcade that surrounds it recalls the Roman peristyle garden.

The reconquest of Spain and Portugal did not signal the end of Islamic influence on gardens (or architecture), because *mudéjar* styles are in some measure a continuation of earlier Islamic forms. The term *mudéjar,* a Hispanized corruption of an Arabic word meaning 'domesticated' or 'subjugated', was used to denote both Muslims who remained in Spain after the Reconquista and a style of architecture and decorative art that developed during the 12th to 15th centuries and remained influential thereafter.

In architecture, including garden architecture, the term initially referred to work executed by Moorish craftsmen for Spanish masters, but later came to denote a hybrid Moorish style (sometimes combining Gothic structures with Moorish decorative elements) that could be adopted by any designer or craftsman. At the level of garden design (and in other arts), the *mudéjar* style meant that Moorish design was not abandoned, but rather assimilated into Christian art.

In garden art, one example is the gardens of the Alcázar in Seville, which fell to Christian forces in 1248. The Alcázar was built by Pedro the Cruel a century later. The *mudéjar* style of the original building and gardens can be glimpsed in the Patio de las Doncellas (Courtyard of the Maidens), of which the upper level is a Renaissance addition, but the lower level is a survival from

5. Garden of the Alcázar in Córdoba, Spain.

Pedro's building, and the garden (once paved with marble) has been restored, and now has a large water tank flanked by sunken gardens. Similarly, the recent rebuilding of the gardens of the Alcázar in Córdoba (see Figure 5) has recovered many Islamic elements, including the terraces, long pools, and walkways.

Perhaps the most enduring legacy of the Islamic garden in Spain is the courtyard (Spanish *patio*). The Palacio de Viana in Córdoba, for example, is a 16th-century palace that has been continuously modified and extended throughout its history. It now has twelve courtyards ranging from the 16th century to the 20th, and most connect with the rooms of the building that encompasses them. Some are meant to be viewed from within the house, and one, the Patio de las Rejas (Courtyard of the Bars), built in 1624, can be seen through ironwork from the street, so demonstrating the power and wealth and standing of the family to passers-by (see Figure 6).

The Islamic Golden Age is conventionally deemed to extend from the 8th century to the 13th, but the Mughal gardens of the

6. Patio de las Rejas, Palacio de Viana, Córdoba, Spain.

Indian subcontinent and the Moorish gardens of Spain extend that period much closer to the present, and are a horticultural reminder of the greatness of Islamic civilization.

Chapter 3
The East Asian garden

China

The history of the garden in China poses two challenges for Westerners. The first is scale: the garden tradition is 2,000 years old, and has never stood still. The second is that the Chinese eye sees the garden through the prism of a set of philosophical assumptions and values that differ from those through which Westerners view gardens. The three contending (and sometimes interpenetrating) worldviews pertinent to Chinese garden history are Confucianism, Daoism, and Buddhism.

Confucianism originated in the 6th century BCE as an ethical system centred on the question of how people should deal with each other, and its notion of cultivation of the self is well suited to the cognate idea of cultivation of the garden. Daoism (so spelt in Pinyin; formerly spelt Taoism), which emerged in the 4th century BCE, has a similarly ethical orientation, to which is added an obligation to live in harmony with the Dao, the principle underlying life. Daoism is also characterized by a respect for the 'immortals' (those who have achieved immortality), by a life disciplined with a view to achieving longevity or immortality, and by respect for the natural world. Buddhism, which centres on a quest for enlightenment and immortality, was introduced to China (from India) in the 5th century CE by the Wei rulers of northern China. Its disciplines of self-examination and meditation and its notion of sacred space (especially groves of trees) have given Buddhism strong links with gardens. In its Zen variation, Buddhism became an important ideological influence in Japanese gardens.

All of these (non-theistic) religions affect the design and the use of gardens in China, and intertwined with these religious influences there are shared cultural conventions, some of great antiquity. The house was often separate from the garden, and a distinction was made between the order imposed by domestic architecture and the freedom to be enjoyed in the garden—even a garden that contained buildings. There was an aspiration to create an idealized nature in the garden, one in which the underlying principles of order were not readily apparent.

When a version of this idea arrived in Europe in the 18th century, it had been current in China for millennia. In practice this idea meant that the structural elements in the design of the garden were not obvious, so the spatial relations between the elements of the constructed landscape had to be inferred. There was also an associative element in the garden, so movement by the visitor within the garden would produce a variety of perspectives that had correlatives in the mental state of the observer; this was sometimes expressed as an alignment of feelings (*qing*) and scenery (*jing*). Finally, there was a wholly unforced sense of representation in the garden. This was partly a sense of the garden as a microcosm of the kingdom or the wider world, but it also enabled viewers to see artfully arranged natural objects in the garden, such as a stone in a lake or in a dry garden, as representing a particular geographical feature that might be real or mythical. Gardens often contain an emblem of the microcosm in the form of an area reserved for miniature trees planted in trays, a practice known as *pencai* ('tray planting') or *penjing* ('tray scenery'), which is usually designated in the West as bonsai, its Japanese name.

The notion of what constitutes a garden in China reflects a cultural tradition quite different from that of the West. The small garden in the West is primarily a place for horticulture, so flowers and grassed lawns are important elements, perhaps with a modest water feature. In the traditional Chinese garden, the herbaceous border does not exist, nor does the lawn—though moss is cultivated in gardens. The emphasis is rather on rocks and water—especially rocks. In Chinese gardens artfully placed rocks represent the earth, and particularly its mountains. There is a mature and sophisticated aesthetics of the appreciation of stones, known in China as *gongshi* or 'scholar's rocks'. Small rocks are usually displayed indoors, sometimes mounted on stands, but outdoor garden rocks are similarly freighted with meaning, and appreciated for their sculptural qualities, their textures, and the colours and patterns of their surfaces. Rocks were not regarded as lifeless, but rather as visible manifestations of energy (*qi*). They are sometimes displayed alone, but are often massed in sculptural groups. Water is the other elemental presence in the Chinese garden, representing in its substance the nurturing of nature and in its stillness the contemplative ideal. The notion of water as the sustainer of nature means that there is no aspiration to clarity in the water of a pond: algae are welcome in the Chinese garden.

If we think of a garden as a designed landscape, and not merely a large space enclosed for hunting, then the garden in China might be deemed to have begun in the Han Period (206 BCE–220 CE), which was broadly contemporary with the Roman Empire in the West. The Han emperor Wudi (141–86 BCE), who instituted Confucianism as the official basis of conduct, created hunting parks, of which the largest was built in a forest west of Xi'an in 138 BCE. Literary sources declared that the park, known as Shang Lin Yuan (Supreme Forest Garden), contained more than thirty palaces, many ponds, thousands of different species of plants, and a menagerie of rare animals. Without archaeological evidence it is difficult to evaluate the exactness of these descriptions, but at the least they represent the ideal of a hunting park that was in some measure realized in Shang Lin Yuan.

It was also during the reign of Wudi that the earliest documented palace garden emerged. The palace and its garden were built in 104 BCE at Chang'an; the site is on the edge of the modern city of Xi'an. There he created a garden with a pond in which there were three small islands that were representations of Penglai, Fangzhang, and Yingzhou, the legendary Daoist islands of the immortals. The symbolism thus embedded in the garden the quest for immortality. Representations of these islands subsequently became a standard feature of imperial and aristocratic gardens. Such gardens were to grow in size and splendour to a scale comparable to Versailles in the West.

Parallel to this grand tradition, there was also a gradual development of relatively small scholars' gardens, of which early examples are documented in literary accounts. The garden near Luoyang of the late 3rd-century writer Shi Chong, which he calls Jing Gu Yuan (Garden of the Golden Valley), featured rockeries, pavilions, and a made-made lake for boating and fishing; there was also an area reserved for agriculture. At the other extreme, some private gardens eschewed splendour in favour of a principled simplicity and rusticity. The garden of the poet Tao Yuanming in Jiangnan, for example, celebrated the ideal of withdrawal from the world of the court (or, in his case, the army) to a life of solitude conducive to the composition of poetry.

China was for centuries divided between a Buddhist northern dynasty and a southern Confucian dynasty. Thereafter the country was reunited under the Sui Dynasty (581–618). Yangdi, the penultimate Sui emperor, created a vast garden (destroyed when the Sui were overthrown) that was invariably described in improbable superlatives that promoted the idea of the garden as an embodiment of imperial excess: it was said to have been created by a million workers, many of whom died in the process;

in winter the bare deciduous trees were draped in silk flowers; richly apparelled automata mounted in boats performed seventy-two scenes from Chinese history.

The consolidation of China under the short-lived Sui Dynasty formed a solid foundation for the succeeding Tang Dynasty (618–906), during which China emerged as one of the world's great empires. The art and literature of 8th-century China are conventionally regarded as the high-water mark of Chinese civilization, and set the standards against which later poets and artists measured themselves. In the Tang Period, petrophilia—the love of stones—evolved into a structured appreciation of rocks, which were valued for their thinness (*shou*), surface texture (*zhou*), openness (*tou*), and perforations (*lou*). Buildings became a more prominent presence in the garden, and indeed began to define the structural organization of the garden.

On the horizontal plane, structural form was united in part by pathways and waterways, but also by visual perspectives. Upper floors in buildings facilitated new perspectives, including broader vistas within the walls and enhanced views of the 'borrowed scenery' (*jie jing*) beyond the walls. The capacity for viewing was enlarged by walls consisting of open latticework. Glimpsed views through such openings created the illusion of a large space, as did constantly turning paths. Elevation, even of a single storey, represented a greater proximity to the immortals, and so became a place for contemplation. It was this thinking, rooted in Daoism, that underlay the later convention of the garden owner's library being accommodated in an upstairs room in the garden.

Three outstanding gardens typify the design of the Tang Dynasty. The poet, musician, painter, and civil servant Wang Wei had a country estate called Wangchuan Nieye (Wang River Estate), landscaped *c.*742 on a site in the foothills of the Qin Mountains near Chang'an. Our knowledge of the garden derives chiefly from Wang's twenty poems on the subject, describing structures such as terraces, bridges, garden buildings (mostly pavilions), and walled compounds as well as areas set aside for agriculture.

Li Deyu was a poet and statesman who, *c.*825, laid out an estate called Pingquan Shanzhuang (Ping River Mountain Estate) south of Luoyang, in Henan Province. It was conceived on an altogether larger scale than Wang Wei's garden. Whereas Wang had some twenty structures within his estate, Li had more than one hundred buildings, including many pavilions, and a large collection of rocks and rare trees that became the subject of his collection of 'Eleven miscellaneous poems written as I thought of the rocks and trees of Pingquan'. The garden was conceived as an act of filial piety, in that Li was fulfilling the wish of his late father, but Li's frequent and protracted absences meant that it gradually came to represent the remembrance of an ideal world. The collecting of rocks became an obsession for Li, and the depth of his petrophilia was sometimes censured by poets of later generations.

In contrast to the estates of Wang and Li, in 817 the poet Bai Juyi built a small garden called Cao Tang (Thatched Hall) on Mount Lu, Jiangxi Province. The unpainted wooden building that gave the garden its name was designed partly to provide shelter from sun and rain, but also to facilitate views of the terraced garden with its waterfall and pond. The austerity of the building (of which a replica has been built on the site), which is emphasized in poems such as 'Mountain Dwelling', reflects both the poet's Buddhist ideals and the conditions of his exile from the court.

The advent of the Song Dynasty in 960 heralded important cultural changes, including the displacement of governance by the hereditary land-owning aristocracy in favour of rule by a trained class of scholar-officials, many of whom had small private retreats with gardens. Scholar-officials employed scholar-artists who memorialized the rocks and ancient trees of private retreats. The best known private garden of this period is Dule Yuan (The Garden of Solitary Happiness), which was built in 1073 near

Luoyang by the scholar-official Sima Guang. In an essay on his garden Sima Guang emphasized its sufficiency, noting that a wren in the woods requires only a single branch on which to perch. The extent to which the layout of the garden can be discerned through later literary accounts is limited, but it is clear that it contained at least five pavilions, one of which was fashioned as a fisherman's hut and another as Sima Guang's library, and that the structural elements included waterways.

The Yuan Dynasty (1271–1368) was a period of foreign conquest, during which China was absorbed into the vast Mongol Empire established by Kublai Khan and ruled by a series of Mongol khans. The best known Yuan garden was the enclosed park at Kublai Khan's summer palace at Xanadu (now Shangdu, in Inner Mongolia), revealed to the West by Marco Polo and immortalized in English poetry by Coleridge. Marco's stories include a brief account of the park, which is said to contain fountains, rivers and streams, and beautiful meadows. The site of Xanadu survives as a ruin, but apart from waterworks, nothing of the garden remains above ground. Some features of a Yuan garden can be discerned in the Lion Forest (or Lion Grove) Garden in Suzhou (west of Shanghai), where nine of more than fifty gardens enjoy UNESCO World Heritage status. The garden was built by Zen Buddhist monks in 1342. The craggy artificial mountains erected that year are still in place, and the paths along their wooded slopes may well follow their original courses.

The Ming Dynasty (1368–1644) marked a restoration of Chinese rule and the imposition of a courtly style on the painters of the period. Court artists were required to produce landscapes and other set pieces (e.g. of birds and flowers) that would project the approved image of the court as virtuous and benevolent. Some of these painters also designed gardens, and their gardens mimicked some of the techniques of painting, so the composition of rock gardens became a reflection of the painting technique known as *cunfa*, in which light ink strokes are used to evoke texture. The art of the garden thus recapitulated the art of the painting, and so the notion of composition became as important to the garden as it always had been in painting.

In the 16th century some of these painterly garden designers began to travel from site to site, and gradually they emerged as professional garden designers, working independently of the court on the small private gardens that are characteristic of the period. The small scale of these gardens meant that the traditional ideas of the capacious imperial garden, such as the notion of the garden as a microcosm, became increasingly symbolic and less representational. As such abstractions are not immediately accessible, there arose a tradition of naming garden features, and increasingly the names bore both the burden of representation and the suggestion of meaning. Gourds or vases intimated an aspiration to longevity, so a feature named after (or shaped like) a gourd or a vase would represent that aspiration (see Figure 7).

The best known extant gardens of the Ming Dynasty are in Suzhou. Examples of 16th- and early 17th-century gardens in the city (all subsequently modified) include two of China's most famous gardens, the Lingering Garden and the Humble Administrator's Garden. The large Lingering Garden (so named in 1876) is dominated by its buildings, which are connected by a winding covered walkway some 700 metres long. Its features include a stone forest (substantially augmented in the early 19th century) with a fine collection of scholar's rocks. The eponym of the Humble Administrator's Garden was Wang Xianchen, a government official who devoted his retirement to his garden, which is the largest in Suzhou. The garden contains a substantial lake (with an island shaped like a boat) planted with lotus, and several smaller ponds. The central part of the garden attempts to recreate in miniature the scenery of the Lower Yangtze, including forested hills topped by pavilions.

7. Vase-shaped opening in Yu Garden (Yuyuan), Shanghai, 1557–9.

The Qing Dynasty (1644–1911) of the Manchus shifted the cultural centre of China northwards. The best known of the extant imperial gardens of the period is the garden of the Summer Palace (Yihe yuan) in Beijing, on which construction began in 1750. Remarkably, most of its area is given over to a large lake. The principal feature of the garden is Longevity Hill, of which the portion nearer the lake consists of buildings—palaces, temples, monasteries (lamaseries), towers, pavilions, and bridges—laid out on both sides of a central axis. Along the shore there is a white marble balustrade, behind which is the famous covered gallery—a mile long—with 273 bays. Many of the buildings are oriented to facilitate distant views of borrowed landscapes, so a huge garden is made to seem even larger. The lake has three large islands, corresponding on an imperial scale to the tiny islands of the immortals to be found in private gardens.

The private gardens of the Qing Dynasty are characterized by regional variations. The relatively small private imperial garden at the north end of the Forbidden City in Beijing, for example, has an axial layout, whereas the Qing scholar gardens in Suzhou have designs that are more responsive to the contours of the landscape. The innovative Couple's Retreat Garden, for example, is laid out on either side of residential accommodation, but the two sides are not symmetrical. Similarly, the Retreat and Reflection Garden, which was built by a painter, is centred on a pool, but there is no axis controlling the layout of garden features. Indeed, the view from the Gathering Beauty Pavilion in the north-west corner resembles a painting of buildings in a natural landscape.

The loss of imperial patronage during the Republican Period (1912–49) and of private property under the People's Republic (1949–present) has meant that new gardens have not been commissioned and existing gardens have either fallen into dereliction or been taken into public ownership.

Japan

The origins of the spiritualized landscapes of Japanese gardens lie in Shinto, the native religion of Japan. In antiquity this was not an organized religion, but rather a diverse set of folk beliefs and ritual practices. In place of gods, there were spirits (*kami*) deemed to reside in the natural world and in the revered dead. The first gardens in Japan seem to have been the enclosed ground around Shinto shrines erected at sacred outcrops and groves; the ground was covered in white sand or small stones to signify cleansing. This animistic spirituality has continued to be an important strain in Japanese culture up to the present, and has informed garden design and the Japanese experience of the garden for centuries.

The advent of the Asuka period (538–710 CE), which marks the beginning of documented Japanese history, saw the arrival in Japan of Buddhism and Daoism from China and Korea. Daoism offered clear synergies with Shinto beliefs. The Shinto imperative to live in harmony with the spirits embodied in the natural world easily accommodated the Daoist aspiration to live in harmony with the Dao, the principle underlying the natural world. Daoist mythology also began to appear in Japanese gardens, so Penglai, Fangzhang, and Yingzhou (the Daoist islands of the immortals) became Hōrai, Hōjō, and Eishū, and could be represented in miniature by rocks or islands or mounds.

The naming of stones and the planting of lotus reflected the traditions of Pure Land Buddhism, which is represented in the reconstructed Pure Land Buddhist gardens at Jōruri-ji and Mōtsū-ji. Another early element in the Japanese garden was the Chinese aesthetic of the appreciation of stones (*aiseki*); small stones, known as *suiseki*, are analogous to Chinese scholar's rocks. No early Japanese garden survives, but the evidence of poetry and archaeology suggests that many elements of the Japanese pond garden, with its constituent elements of stones, water, and horticulture, were in place by the 8th century.

In 794 a new capital was established in Heian-kyo ('capital of peace and tranquillity'), which has been known since the 11th century as Kyoto. It was in Kyoto, which was destined to remain the imperial capital until 1868, that secular and religious architecture, literature, painting, music, and the decorative arts were to create a distinctive national style. All phases in Japan's garden history are represented in the city's gardens, which since the late 19th century have had a global influence on garden design.

The early gardens of Kyoto, including those of the imperial palace on the northern edge of city, survive only in literary accounts. The balance between horticulture and gravelled surfaces in the imperial palace is striking: the steps to the throne hall, for example, were flanked by two fruit trees (mandarin orange and cherry, representing the Chinese and Japanese strains in the culture of Kyoto), and otherwise the ground was covered with white gravel, a pattern reminiscent of Shinto shrines.

Private Kyoto gardens before the 13th century clearly reflect a debt to China: in laying out the gardens, the principles of geomancy were observed, and typically there is a pond in the centre, around which are ranged pavilions linked by covered walkways. Symbolic rocks were another important feature. Pure Land Buddhist temples also had pond gardens, often stocked with lotus, the flower that symbolized reincarnation in the Pure Land. The principal Buddha in Pure Land Buddhism is Amitabha (known in Japan as Amida), and ponds were sometimes shaped as the first letter in his name (अ) in the Devanagari script.

In the 13th century, Zen Buddhism took root in Japan, brought by Chinese monks fleeing the Mongol invasion, and Zen gradually became an important presence in the garden. Whereas Pure Land Buddhism was visionary and otherworldly, Zen was centred on meditation, and celebrated manual labour and the cultivation of simplicity and personal discipline. Temple gardens thus become settings for meditation, and the labour of gardening—raking gravel as well as tending plants—became one of the routes to enlightenment (*satori*).

Early Zen temples were built in remote locations, often on the wooded slopes of mountains. By the end of the 15th century, however, Zen temples had begun to be built near towns and cities. The forest temples had been integrated into their mountainous settings, but in the much smaller urban temples, the mountains and the forests were represented symbolically, and the idea of the garden became cerebral and abstracted. During this period the earliest examples of the dry landscape (*karesansui*, 'dry mountain and water') garden appear. These gardens were laid out in front of the abbot's residence (*hōjō*) in Zen temple complexes.

The most famous of these dry landscape *hōjō* gardens is the Ryōan-ji Garden in Kyoto, the date of which is uncertain: it is possible that its origins lie in the temple complex constructed in 1488, but it is perhaps more likely that in its present form it dates from the mid-17th century. The garden consists of a flat rectangle of gravel that is raked every day by the monks. The garden contains fifteen stones, grouped in five clusters: one of five stones, two of three stones, and two of two stones. Each cluster is bordered by moss that constitutes the only vegetation in the garden. The meaning of the layout is unknown, but that has not inhibited generations of tour guides from offering detailed explanations to the tourists seated on the veranda of the *hōjō*, often observing that only fourteen stones are visible at one time, and explaining that all fifteen can only be observed by those who have attained enlightenment. That idea is undocumented, and may be no more than a speculation hallowed by age.

In the same period that the dry landscape garden began to appear in Zen temples all over Japan, the gardens associated with the tea ceremony (*chanoyu*) began to emerge. Tea had been drunk in Japan for centuries, but its ritualistic consumption in the tea ceremony is a development of the 15th century. This was the Muromachi Period (1392–1573), so named for the district in Kyoto where the Ashikaga clan lived. The origins of the tea ceremony lie in the private gardens of the Ashikaga, and the preparation and serving of tea are only one aspect of a capacious Zen intellectual aesthetic of *chanoyu* that also embraced architecture, the decorative arts (including interior design, painting, flower arranging, and calligraphy), and garden design.

In the early Muromachi Period tea was served by attendants as the host sat with his guests in a pavilion overlooking the garden; there is a surviving example of such a pavilion in the Dōjinsai of the Tōgudō in Kyoto, which was built in 1486 for purposes that included the tea ceremony. In the later Muromachi Period, however, the attendants were displaced by the host, who made the tea and served it to his guests. The small tea room of this period had to be approached through the garden, which was designed to prepare guests for the tea ceremony by instilling a contemplative spirit in the approaching visitor, whose steps were artfully slowed by the need to navigate a winding footpath consisting of irregularly shaped stepping stones placed at irregular intervals. Ceremonies were often held at sunrise or sunset, so visitors were guided through the gloom by lanterns on the side of the path. The path wound so that the visitor could experience a programme of differing views that would produce corresponding emotions, rather like the associative gardens of 18th-century England. The ritual ablutions required before the ceremony could be conducted at a stone basin known as a *tsukubai*, from which water could be lifted with a bamboo ladle.

The cultural creativity of the Muromachi Period was brought to a halt by the warfare of the Momoyama Period (1573–1603), and when peace was restored under the feudal government of the Tokugawa Shogunate in what is known as the Edo Period

(1603–1867), the cultural landscape of Japan was transformed. Foreigners were expelled as part of a policy of isolation, and in the absence of foreign influence, Japan turned inwards, reviving and refining its native cultural traditions. One exception to this policy of isolation was that a community of Chinese monks was allowed to settle at Manpuku-ji, near Kyoto. This community proved to be a conduit for Ming literati painting, in which the calligraphic representation of thin trees was replicated in the bonsai cultivated in Japanese Edo gardens.

The military rulers of Japan during this period extended their patronage to both the former imperial court and the Buddhist establishment. As a result, the gardens of imperial palaces and Buddhist temples were rejuvenated, and the new rulers built ostentatious palaces for themselves, complete with magnificent gardens. The finest survival from the 17th century is the pond garden of the shogunal Ninomaru Palace within the Nijō Castle complex in Kyoto. This garden, one of many designed by the early 17th-century architect and tea master Kobori Enshū, is centred on a vaguely rectangular pond edged by boulders and bordered by pavilions from which the garden can be viewed. The planting is now mixed, but was originally wholly coniferous.

Kobori Enshū's gardens (and other gardens laid out in his style) embody features from earlier Japanese traditions, such as the islands of the immortals in the pond and a highly developed aesthetics of stones. Other features develop rather than reproduce earlier traditions. The pavilions, for example, are merely resting places in gardens in which visitors are expected to be moving. The notion, originating in the tea garden, of a slow walk past varied scenery, evolves into the idea of the stroll garden focused on the emotions of the peripatetic visitor whose perambulations are guided by footpaths. The Japanese term *kaiyū*, which is normally translated as 'stroll garden' or 'promenade garden', has the literal sense of a garden with many pleasures, which means that strolling is a means of experiencing a carefully planned sequence of vistas that will constantly stimulate, reflect, and refract the changing emotions of the visitor. In some cases the vistas are designed to prompt recollections of poems. The twenty-one-acre Rikugien ('six virtues') Garden in Tokyo, for example, is a stroll garden in which the visitor experiences views of eighty-eight miniature gardens, each of which is intended to evoke a traditional Japanese poem.

Another feature of traditional gardens elaborated in the Edo Period was the borrowed landscape (*shak-kei*), which in earlier periods usually referred to views of mountains over walls, but was developed in the 17th century into landscapes designed to frame distant features and so incorporate them into the garden. The Rikugien Garden in Tokyo has artificial mounds from which Mount Fuji can be viewed, and several monastery gardens around Kyoto have features that frame views of Mount Hiei. Such views were spiritually charged. Mount Fuji had long been a sacred mountain, and because it was relatively close (100 km) to Edo (now Tokyo) it became an important symbolic presence in the Edo Period. The woodblock prints of Katsushika Hokusai, 'Thirty-Six Views of Mount Fuji', include Japan's most famous print, the *Great Wave*. Similarly, Mount Hiei was associated with the temple of Enryaku-ji, the ancient monastery where Tendai Mahayana Buddhism was first established in Japan.

In the Meiji Period (1868–1912), Japan was once again opened to outside influences, and gardens in that period are a blend of Japanese and Western influences. The Meiji Shrine in Tokyo, for example, retains Japanese features such as a programme of vistas, but its planting is in part Westernized, notably in the iris beds that are the best known feature of the gardens.

The first half of the 20th century in Japan was dominated by conflicts extending from the Russo-Japanese War to World War II. The post-war period, however, has seen an extraordinary cultural renewal in which garden design is one of many elements.

Globalization has entailed both influence from the world beyond Asia and the spread of some strains of Japanese culture around the world. The most striking of the inward influences is the practice of gardening: indeed, 'gardening' has become a loanword in Japanese.

In the past, cultural elites employed gardeners, but now vast garden centres proliferate all over the country, and gardening has become a leisure activity. Many domestic gardens retain traditional features, but others incorporate elements from Western traditions. A new generation of garden designers, many of whom do not come from a traditional gardening background, has revived earlier styles in new settings such as hotels and rooftop gardens. Koki Fukaya, a contemplative designer with an interest in what he called 'inner landscape design', created the landscape (which he called the 'outer space') of the Keio Plaza Hotel in Tokyo. Similarly, the rooftop garden wrapped around the fourth-floor reception area of the Canadian Embassy in Tokyo was designed by Shunmyo Masuno in a *karesansui* (dry landscape) style.

Japanese gardens have also become an important cultural export, and can be seen all over the world. Those created by Japanese designers, such as Ishihara Kazuyuki's Edo Garden at the Chelsea Flower Show in 2015, typically attend to the styles of a particular period. Non-Japanese designers often cheerfully combine features from different periods, and readily adapt plantings to differing soils and climates. Many Japanese gardens around the world are peace gardens, and so reflect the repudiation of militarism in post-war Japan. It is striking that a disproportionate number of such gardens are in the United States, which was once Japan's enemy. The antiquity and complexity of Japanese culture are little understood in the West, and so Japanese gardens in Western countries form a welcoming point of access to one of the world's great civilizations.

Chapter 4
Italy

The Renaissance

The renaissance of gardening in Tuscany was inaugurated by Leon
Battista Alberti's publication of *De re aedificatoria* ('On the art
of building') in 1452. The garden of the Villa Quaracchi, which
was built by Giovanni Rucellai in about 1459, contains various
medieval elements (arbours, pergolas, and a rose garden), but it
conforms in so many respects to the principles enunciated by
Alberti that its design has been confidently attributed to him. The
house was built on a small hill, as Alberti had recommended, and
the axis of the garden was extended beyond the *giardino segreto*
('secret garden', a small private garden) along a tree-lined avenue
to the River Arno. Box and scented evergreens amenable to clipping
were planted and shaped into hedges and figures, apparently in
imitation of the 1st-century gardens of Pliny the Younger. The
absence of statues in the Quaracchi gardens may be another
gesture towards Pliny, who eschewed statues in favour of features
constructed out of plants and soil.

Quaracchi had a central axis, and in that respect anticipated the
structure of later gardens, but the garden was designed
independently of the house. The transition from separate designs
for house and garden to fully integrated designs can be seen in
two gardens designed by Michelozzo di Bartolomeo. In about 1451

Michelozzo laid out a garden at Il Trebbio, the Medici hunting lodge at Cafaggiolo; the garden is a walled rectangle detached from the house. A lunette by Giusto Utens shows that the garden was laid out in eight square beds of flowers and vegetables; it was originally bounded by vine pergolas (one of which survives with its original brick columns), and the enclosure blocks out the views. This inwardness is a medieval feature; Il Trebbio is the last of the great medieval gardens of Tuscany.

In 1458 Michelozzo began work on the Medici villa at Fiesole, and there he constructed open gardens on two terraces. The house opens out directly onto the upper terrace, which overlooks Florence in the valley below; the enclosure has shrunk to a *giardino segreto*, which still survives. In this design the essential features of the 16th-century Italian Renaissance garden are seen in embryo. They were to be fully realized in Rome in the Belvedere Court and the Villa Madama. It was these Roman buildings, and others now lost, that became the model for garden design in Tuscany.

Sixteenth-century Italian gardens were fully integrated with the houses to which they were attached, and retained the use of terraces with attractive views. To this late 15th-century outline, designers added four distinctive features that were to influence gardens all over the world: symmetry, statues, water, and a balance between constructed and natural materials.

The first garden to have a symmetrical layout around a central axis was Niccolò Tribolo's garden at the Medici villa at Castello. Tribolo subsequently laid out the Boboli Gardens in accordance with the same principle. The terraces of Italian gardens often contained springs that provided natural sources of water, and in some gardens aqueducts and conduits were used to ensure a constant supply of water under pressure. Some gardens, such as the Villa Lante, the Villa d'Este at Cernobbio (on Lake Como), the Villa Cicogna (near Milan), and the Villa Farnese at Caprarola, have water staircases or water contained within sculpted channels (*catene d'acqua*, literally 'chains of water') flanked by dry staircases, and Frascati villas such as Villa Aldobrandini and Villa Mondragone had water theatres. Water was also used to power *giochi d'acqua* ('water games') that sprayed unsuspecting visitors; such devices may be loftily dismissed as childish, but they delighted visitors for several centuries, and are still capable of doing so.

The sculptor Baccio Bandinelli decreed that *le cose che si murano debbono essere guidi e superiori a quelle che si piantano* ('that which is constructed should be the model and master of that which is planted'). This principle was implemented in every major Italian garden of the 16th century. The shape of the garden was outlined with galleries (modelled on the ancient Roman cryptoporticus, a portico enclosed by solid walls with windows), covered walks, and staircases, and fountains were placed at focal points. The interpenetration of house and garden was often achieved by having elements of the house extended into the garden, as at Villa Giulia (built for Pope Julius III in Rome, now the National Etruscan Museum). Gardens were furnished with pavilions, and many contained elaborate grottoes. In some gardens, ornamental pavilions (*casini*) were built in *giardini segreti*, of which the finest surviving example is at the Villa Farnese.

The gardens of classical antiquity were furnished with statues. The first garden to revive this tradition was the Belvedere Court in the Vatican, which contained a collection of ancient statues. Statues modelled on those of antiquity soon began to adorn the fountains at the focal point of gardens such as the Medici villa at Castello and the Palazzo Doria Principe in Genoa. The most bizarre garden with respect to sculptures is the Villa Orsini in Bomarzo (see Figure 8), where monstrous statues were carved out of rock outcrops by unknown sculptors working between 1552 and 1585. They produced an extraordinary range of colossal sculptures, including a temple (one of the few conventionally built

8. Monstrous Orcus mouth, Bomarzo, Italy.

structures), a leaning house, Etruscan urns, masks, giant humans, naturalistic animals such as elephants and tortoises, and many monsters. Unlike other Renaissance gardens, the layout is not symmetrical, because the stone was carved wherever it was found. Indeed, the garden was not laid out, and may not have had an architect, but was instead constructed adventitiously around natural outcrops of volcanic rock protruding from the valley floor. The gardens were virtually unknown before the end of World War II, when they were filmed by Salvador Dalí.

The two best known surviving gardens of 16th-century Italy may be Villa d'Este in Tivoli (to the east of Rome) and the Boboli Gardens in Florence. Villa d'Este was transformed from a Benedictine monastery into a villa for Cardinal Ippolito d'Este, the son of Lucrezia Borgia. The house is a typical Roman villa, but the magnificence of the gardens reduces the house to a supporting role. The gardens were laid out between 1560 and 1575 on a steep slope on the west side of Tivoli. The central axis of the Villa d'Este garden is marked by a grand stairway that climbs from a gateway at the bottom of the garden across a series of majestic terraces to the villa. The two lowest terraces descend in staircases from the house and in ramps (*cordonate*) from the hill on the north-west side, which is the source of the water used to such spectacular effect in the garden. The main source of water is a conduit built by Pirro Ligorio to supply water from the River Aniene.

Entry to the garden is now through the house at the top of the hill, but it was designed to be entered from the lowest terrace, at the opposite end. From this perspective, the first water feature was the Fountain of the Organ, which contained a water organ that could imitate the sound of a trumpet and play in harmony. On the next terrace, the Fountain of the Owl featured small birds whose singing was facilitated by the ingenious use of water; when an owl turned towards them to remonstrate with a water-driven hoot, the birds fell silent. On the higher terraces, the finest feature is the Terrace of a Hundred Fountains (see Figure 9), which consists of three magnificent rows of fountains. Throughout the 17th century the gardens were maintained and a few new features added, notably the Fountain of the Bicchierone built in 1660 by Gianlorenzo Bernini.

The Boboli Gardens lie behind the Pitti Palace in Florence. In 1549 the unfinished palace was bought by Eleanor of Toledo, the duchess of Cosimo I de' Medici. Niccolò Tribolo was quickly commissioned to design a garden; he died the following summer, and the work was completed by Bartolomeo Ammanati. The garden was laid out symmetrically around a central axis, in the middle of which is a U-shaped amphitheatre carved out of a natural hollow in the hill. Below the amphitheatre there is a large courtyard adjoining the palace, and above it is a pond. A painting by Giusto Utens shows that the amphitheatre was thickly planted when he painted it in 1599. There were also parterres laid out at the side of the palace. Immediately behind the palace there was a huge Fountain of Neptune (the Ocean Fountain) by Giambologna; his statue of Ocean is now in the Bargello. Bernardo Buontalenti

9. Terrace of a Hundred Fountains, Villa d'Este, Tivoli.

added a three-chambered grotto (1583–93) filled with statues, the pedestals of which were decorated with sea shells. The first chamber contained four unfinished statues of captives by Michelangelo, intended for the tomb of Julius II and since 1908 in the Accademia. The third chamber, which is the work of Bernardino Pocetti, contains a statue of Venus leaving her bath by Giambologna. Originally this grotto was fitted with *giochi d'acqua* designed by Buontalenti.

In the 17th century the design of the Boboli Gardens was altered considerably. The 17th-century garden, which is the form in which the garden survives today (the only subsequent addition was the *Kaffeehaus* built in 1776), is more monumental than its Renaissance predecessor, but both served the same purpose: the garden was not intended simply to be viewed, but was rather a setting for magnificent spectacles. Events are still mounted there by the Maggio Musicale Fiorentino and it is during such pageants and performances that the purpose of the design is realized.

Italian Renaissance gardens influenced the development of garden design throughout Europe, both in layout and in content. This influence also extended to the proliferation of new species of plants, because the first botanical gardens were in Italy. The purpose of these gardens was to facilitate the study of plants for medicinal purposes. The origins of these gardens are disputed, but they may combine elements of the physic gardens of earlier centuries and the Aztec gardens that the conquistadors had discovered in Mexico.

The Orto Botanico in Pisa (*c.*1543) was planted by Luca Ghini, who taught botany and medicine at the University of Pisa. The garden was planted with medicinal plants gathered by Ghini and his students on field trips in northern Italy. The garden soon developed an international reputation both for the range of its collections and its beauty. It was the first garden in Europe to cultivate the horse chestnut (*Aesculus hippocastanum*), the black walnut (*Juglans nigra*), the ailanthus (*Ailantus glandulosa*), the camphor tree (*Cinnamomum camphora*), the Japanese quince (*Chaenomeles japonica*), the magnolia (*Magnolia grandiflora*), and the tulip tree (*Liriodendron tulipfera*). The garden is still owned by the university, but now specializes in lilies, water lilies, and amaryllis.

The first curator of the botanic garden in Padua was Luigi Squalerno, who had been a pupil of Ghini at Pisa. The garden, which was jointly owned by the University of Padua and the Venetian Republic, was designed by the Bergamese painter Giovanni Batista Moroni and constructed under the supervision of Pietro da Noale (representing the university) and Daniele Barbaro (representing the Venetian Senate). The garden was laid out as an enormous circle, some 90 yards in diameter; the broad outline of the original design has survived, but details of the beds have been changed. The circle was enclosed in 1551, but this wall was replaced in the 18th century by the one that now surrounds the garden. The area within the circle was divided into sixteen equal parts, each of which was divided into four beds. The beds were planted with medicinal herbs, which were used for the instruction of medical students.

Padua was the first garden in Europe to cultivate the potato (*c.*1575), the bignonia (*Bignonia radicans*), the Indian cedar (*Cedrus deodara*), the common acacia (*Robinia pseudoacacia*), the pelargonium (*Pelargonium cuccullatum*), the cyclamen (*Cyclamen persicum*), and the winter jasmine (*Jasminum nudiflorum*), which was rediscovered three centuries later by the Scottish plant collector Robert Fortune.

The 17th and 18th centuries

In the 17th and 18th centuries, Italian gardens continued to be highly structured, with trees in rows and smaller compartments bounded by planting, but many gardens also contained a planted *bosco* in which ground levels were unaltered and trees grew freely. Such gardens were often enriched with buildings and statues in a classical idiom.

The finest surviving 17th-century garden is the Villa Barbarigo at Valsanzibio, in the Veneto near Padua (not to be confused with the Villa Barbarigo that now serves as the town hall of Noventa Vicentina). This baroque garden, formerly known as the Villa Donà dalle Rose, was designed by Luigi Bernini (younger brother of Gianlorenzo) for the Venetian Barbarigo family; it was commissioned in 1665, and completed in 1696. The path from the entrance to the villa garden was conceived as an allegory of man's salvation, but this spiritual intention is expressed in an exuberant display of garden buildings, streams, waterfalls, fountains, and ponds together with a hermit's cave, and some seventy statues set amid trees and shrubs. The statues have moralizing inscriptions on the pedestals. One of the finest features is a large boxwood maze.

The principal influence on the Italian gardens of the 18th century was France. The flatness of French gardens could not be imitated in the hilly landscapes of Italy, but features such as cypress alleys were imitated (e.g. Crivelli Sormani-Verri, in Lombardy), as were radiating structures, which can be seen at gardens such as Villa Pisani and Caserta. Villa Pisani (at Stra, on the Brenta Canal in Veneto), which was rebuilt in a baroque idiom from 1720 to 1735, is too small (eleven hectares) to accommodate a hunting park, but the illusion of one is afforded by the convergence of six rides at a hexagonal archway. The 18th-century garden, which was laid out before the villa was built, was designed by the Paduan architect Girolamo Frigimelica de' Roberti, whose surviving work includes the maze and the original lodges. The long perspectives of the garden reflect French influence (notably Versailles).

The greatest legacy of French influence on the palace gardens of the 18th century is the royal park of King Carlo VII of Naples (later King Carlos III of Spain) at Caserta, north of Naples (see Figure 10). The Palazzo Reale was the work of the architect Luigi Vanvitelli and his son Carlo. Under their supervision the French gardener Martin Biancour laid out an uncompromisingly French garden, aligned along a lengthy axis that extended from the palace to the vast waterfall at the end of the park. On this axis an avenue flanked by *parterres de broderie* (flower beds 'embroidered' with symmetrical designs of box) was extended into a broad canal that leads to the final cascade through fountains embellished with statues. As at Villa Pisani, the hunting park is crossed with radiating hunting rides.

The 19th and 20th centuries

In the late 18th and early 19th centuries the political and economic difficulties of a fragmented Italy meant that many gardens became derelict, and others were converted into low-maintenance *giardini inglesi*. New planting fashions saw the widespread introduction of magnolia, rhododendron, and bougainvillea, much of which spread untrammelled. In the late 19th century, wealthy foreign residents in Italy (mostly British, Anglo-Irish, and American) began to lay out gardens with plants sourced globally rather than locally, sometimes paying little heed to traditional Italian designs. The best known of these collector's gardens is La Mortola, near Ventimiglia on the Ligurian Riviera, which was bought in 1867 by the English businessman Thomas (later Sir Thomas) Hanbury. The garden has some Italian features, such as belvederes, pergolas, statues, and pools, but is at heart designed to display to the greatest possible advantage a remarkable collection of tender plants from all over the world (though one section has been reserved for local plants). These gardens, which are now known as the Giardini Botanici Hanbury, are owned by the University of Genoa, which uses the gardens for

10. Fountain of Venus and Adonis, Palazzo Reale, Caserta.

scientific purposes and maintains the site as one of Europe's finest botanical gardens.

Other expatriates established or restored Renaissance gardens. In 1908 the American heiress Hortense Mitchell bought Villa La Pietra. Together with her English husband, Arthur Acton, she created what is in effect an Anglo-American Renaissance Revival garden in which 'rooms' bounded by plants or built structures are laid out along two axes. Decorative elements include more than 180 statues, arches, and a *teatro de verdura* (a 'green theatre' in which the stage is bounded by clipped hedges). The aesthete Sir Harold Acton inherited La Pietra, and made it a more private place by allowing large trees to obscure views from neighbouring properties. He bequeathed the villa to New York University, which has restored the views intended in the original design.

The most prominent English designer working in early 20th-century Italy was Cecil Pinsent, who restored many derelict gardens for the Anglo-American community, and also designed original gardens in a Renaissance Revival style, including Villa I Tatti in Settignano (for Bernard Berenson), Villa La Foce near Siena (for the writer Iris Origo), and Villa Le Balze in Fiesole (for the philosopher and psychologist Charles Augustus Strong, now restored by Georgetown University).

Since World War II there have been occasional English designers working in Italy (notably Russell Page's La Mortella, in Campania, for Sir William and Lady Walton), but design is now firmly in the hands of Italians. Some of the finest work has been the imaginative restoration of historic gardens, sometimes by the Fondo per l'Ambiente Italiano, which restores historic properties. The past forty years have witnessed the restoration of many Renaissance gardens, including both Villa d'Este gardens and a host of Medici gardens. Among the most prominent historicist designers are Ada Segre, whose scholarly restorations include the *giardini segreti* at Villa Borghese in Rome and the south garden of the Palazzo Doria Pamphili in Genoa, and Giorgio Galletti, whose restorations in the 2010s have included the garden of the Villa Medici (now the Académie de France) in the Villa Borghese, the Garden of Casina Valadier in Rome, and the park of Villa Strozzi in Florence. It is to be hoped that other restorations, such as the water theatres in the Villa Aldobrandini and Villa Mondragone, both in Frascati, will eventually follow.

Chapter 5
France

The Renaissance

French gardens of the Renaissance were influenced but not overwhelmed by the design of Italian gardens. In the early 16th century the Italian elements were usually incidental: at Gaillon, for example, marble fountains were imported from Italy, and at Fontainebleau bronze casts of ancient marbles were brought from Italy. The fundamental design of gardens of this period, however, was rooted in the tradition of the enclosed garden wholly independent of the house rather than in the Italian ideal of the interpenetration of house and garden. There was also an important topographical difference: Italian gardens were usually terraced, but French gardens, with the important exception of the Italianate garden at St-Germain-en-Laye (and the mid-17th-century garden at Vaux-le-Vicomte) tended to be flat. An important consequence of this distinction is that flowing water was a relatively minor feature in French gardens of the 16th century. Until the gardens at Versailles were constructed, French fountains produced mere trickles of water, whereas Italian fountains produced torrents.

The rediscovery of Vitruvius affected garden design in both Italy and France, in that it shifted the conceptual emphasis of the garden from the traditional horticultural stress on fruit, vegetables, and medicinal herbs to an architectural emphasis on form and harmony. In France the dominant architectural features of gardens were pavilions, such as those at Amboise, Blois, and Gaillon, and galleries, such as the monumental wooden gallery at Montargis, the stone gallery at Gaillon, the gallery beyond the moats at Chantilly, and the free-standing painted gallery at Fontainebleau.

In early French estates the house and garden were usually designed independently. The ideal of an integrated design was first achieved by Philibert Delorme, who established at Anet (1546–52) the prerogative of the architect to design the garden as well as the house. A few years later Sebastiano Serlio retrospectively imposed a unified design on Ancy-le-Franc by enclosing both house and garden within a huge rectangular terrace. The influence of the gardens of Roman cardinals, especially the Villa Farnese, ensured the continued life of small gardens set apart from the main house. In the 1550s Cardinal de Bourbon built such a private retreat at Gaillon, constructing a canal, an ornamental pavilion (the Maison Blanche), and a hermitage carved out of a rock; the hermitage may have been purely decorative, but it is also possible that the cardinal installed a hermit-in-residence.

One of the distinctive features of French gardens of the 16th century is the presence of a canal. At Fleury-en-Bière, the first of these canals still survives, and is thought to have inspired the Grand Canal at Fontainebleau; Philibert Delorme subsequently incorporated a canal into the garden at Anet. In the 17th century grand canals were to become an important element in Le Nôtre's gardens at Vaux-le-Vicomte, Chantilly, Maintenon, Sceaux, and Versailles.

Plantings in French gardens were arranged in the flat ornamental flower gardens known as parterres, which were well established by the time Serlio printed designs for geometrical parterres in

L'Architettura (1537). A comparison of this volume to the 1572 edition of *L'agriculture et maison rustique*, by Charles Estienne and Jean Liébault, shows how parterres developed in the intervening half century: in 1537 parterres were individual creations sealed in separate compartments (*compartiments de broderie*), but by 1572 parterres had been integrated into an overall structural plan. Claude Mollet, who traced this development to Anet, designed parterres for Fontainebleau, St-Germain-en-Laye, and the Tuileries; his designs are printed in the *Théâtre d'agriculture* (1600) of Olivier de Serres. The parterre was further developed by Mollet's sons at the Luxembourg Palace in Paris; these early 17th-century parterre designs for royal gardens were collected by Jacques Boyceau in his *Traité du Jardinage* (1638).

The first botanical garden in France was the Jardin des Plantes at Montpellier, which was built by Pierre Richer de Belleval between 1593 and 1607. It is one of the few French examples of a garden with a terraced mount (which still survives). Every plant in the garden was labelled, and 1,332 species and varieties were listed in Richer de Belleval's *Onomatologia* (1598). The garden was destroyed during Richelieu's siege of Montpellier in 1622, and subsequently rebuilt on a smaller scale. In the late 17th century one of the curators was the taxonomist Pierre Magnol, the eponym of the magnolia.

The grand gardens of France, like the Boboli Gardens in Florence, were used as settings for large entertainments, and by the middle of the 16th century gardens had been extended or reshaped to incorporate extensive open areas in which such events could be staged. Such provision is most pronounced in the gardens commissioned or enlarged by Catherine de Médicis at Chenonceaux, Fontainebleau, Montceaux-en-Brie, and, most capaciously, at the Tuileries. Many French Renaissance gardens have disappeared, but the drawings of Jacques Ducerceau record the châteaux and gardens of France in the 1560s and 1570s; his drawings also include plans for châteaux and gardens that were never executed.

The 17th century

The apogee of French garden art is the 17th-century formal garden known as the *jardin à la française*, of which the greatest and most influential exponent was André Le Nôtre. The *jardin à la française* is characterized by geometry: a central axis defines the symmetrical layout of trees, shrubs, paths, flower beds, ponds, canals, and statues. The gardens are typically designed to be seen from a terrace, and the viewer's perspective is often corrected by trapezoidal parterres and gradually widening aisles. The vocabulary of such gardens is strikingly architectural, so gardens are said to have halls (*salles*), rooms (*chambres*), aisles (*allées*), walls (*murs*) of hedging, theatres of greenery (*théâtres de verdure*), and water stairs (*escaliers*). Similarly, there are analogies to soft furnishings and fabrics such as floor mats (*tapis de pelouse*), trimmed curtains (*rideaux*), embroidered boxwood (*brodés de buis*), and embroidered parterres (*parterres de broderie*).

André Le Nôtre was the most distinguished member of a dynasty of royal gardeners. His first independent project was the garden of the château of Vaux-le-Vicomte (south-east of Paris), which was built for Nicolas Fouquet, Louis XIV's minister of finance. It was Fouquet who brought together for the first time the creators of the Louis XIV style: Louis Le Vau (the architect), Charles Le Brun (the painter, decorator, and designer), and Le Nôtre (the garden designer); this was the team that was later to work together at Versailles. The architecture of the garden complements that of the château, and each was designed with vantage points for viewing the other. The château, which has a symmetrical design, is placed on an axis that leads past *parterres de broderie* to a cross-axial canal, beyond which lies a huge copy of the Farnese Hercules. In the distance, *allées* radiate into the woods.

Versailles was the principal residence of Louis XIV, and later became the seat of government. In 1661 Louis XIV began to enlarge the château, and Le Nôtre assumed responsibility for the design and layout of the gardens. Le Nôtre's starting point was a garden with avenues and parterres that had been laid out in the 1630s. The central axis extended to the west from what is now the central window of the Hall of Mirrors. Le Nôtre lengthened the perspective by constructing the Grand Canal, and thereafter the line followed by the eye began with gravel, which in turn gave way to lawn (the Tapis Vert) and eventually to the water of the canal and the horizon. This axis, together with parallel axes on either side, is intersected by four cross-axial avenues. The grid squares created by the intersections were filled by Le Nôtre and his protégé (and eventual rival) Jules Hardouin-Mansart with ornamental groves (bosquets) and fountains. The sculpture in the gardens was the responsibility of Charles Le Brun. The solar imagery of the sculptures articulated in lead and marble (and later in bronze) the idea of Louis XIV as the Roi Soleil (Sun King). The idea of the outdoor sculpture garden first seen in the ancient statues in the Belvedere Court in the Vatican was realized in Versailles on a grand scale. The buildings in the garden included an *orangerie*, a grand *ménagerie*, and the celebrated Grotto of Tethys.

The reshaping of the landscape was a colossal task, and thousands of men, moving soil in wheelbarrows and plants from all over France in carts, took forty years to complete the garden. The engineering work necessary for the elaborate waterworks in the garden included sourcing water from the Seine and Eure, which in turn required the construction of a series of waterwheels with sufficient power to pump 6,000 cubic metres a day into the gardens. The canal was furnished with a naval flotilla that had no value for defence, but was rather a demonstration of splendour.

In 1668, six years after work on the principal garden had begun, Louis XIV bought the adjoining estate of Trianon, and quickly set about adapting it to his purposes, which centred on his wish to mount grand entertainments. Louis XV, on reaching his majority, entertained elsewhere, but he did take an interest in the garden that reflected mid-18th-century fashion: he extended the gardens to the north-east, initially with formal features and, further away from the Trianon, a farm, a botanic garden, and a new *ménagerie*. In the 1760s the king constructed an elegant pavilion in the gardens; the original Trianon became the Grand Trianon and the new building the Petit Trianon.

On acceding to the throne in 1774, Louis XVI presented the Petit Trianon to his consort, Marie Antoinette, who promptly embarked on a remodelling of the gardens. With the help of her architect, Richard Mique, the queen laid out the gardens of the Petit Trianon in *le style anglo-chinois*. Mique's buildings for the gardens included a Théâtre de la Reine (where the queen staged productions in which members of the royal family performed), a *belvédère* overlooking a small lake, a Temple de l'Amour on an island in a river, and, in an extension of the garden, a *hameau* (hamlet) consisting of a ring of peasant houses around a small lake. The Grange (a rustic ballroom) and the *laiterie* have disappeared, but most of these faux-peasant buildings have survived, a mute testament to the urge to create an Arcadian idyll in which the queen and her family and attendants could assume pastoral roles without the inconvenience of living alongside real peasants.

The 18th century

The gardens of Versailles and Trianon set the standard for the formal and symmetrical *jardin à la française*, but as they developed, they also reflected and sometimes inaugurated new fashions in 18th-century French garden design. The principal innovations, which were often secondary gardens alongside the *jardin à la française*, were the *jardin anglo-chinois*, the *ferme ornée*, the *fabrique*, and the *jardin anglais*.

The *jardin anglo-chinois* was the horticultural strand of *chinoiserie*, a decorative style that was also manifested in ceramics, furniture, textiles, architecture, and interior decoration. The precursor of the style was the Trianon de Porcelaine at Versailles, built in 1670, demolished in 1687, and then replaced by the Trianon de Marbre now on the site. The buildings of the Trianon de Porcelaine were decorated externally with Delft tiles in a Chinese style, and their roofs were constructed and decorated in a Chinese idiom. The style was revived *c.*1739 with the Chinese-style Pavilion of the *Trèfle* at Lunéville, and came back into fashion on a large scale in the late 18th century, in part because of the advocacy of William Chambers's *Designs of Chinese Buildings* (1757; French translation, 1776). Pagodas were erected at Chanteloup (Indre-et-Loire) and Rambouillet, and a fine Chinese house (now destroyed) was built at the Désert de Retz (near Marly, Yvelines).

The term *ferme ornée* was coined by the English landscape designer Stephen Switzer in his *Ichnographia rustica* (1718); 'ichnography' is the science of ground plans. The phrase denotes an ornamented farm, but some examples barely function as farms, and so might better be described as ornamental farms. The term is first mentioned in France in Claude-Henri Watelet's *Essai sur les jardins* in 1774; Watelet's Moulin Joli, on the Seine between Colombes and Argenteuil, was in part a *ferme ornée*. The *hameaux* at Chantilly (1773) and at the Petit Trianon are a related form, but neither was a working farm. In France as in England, the *ferme ornée* was more often discussed than built. The principal French precedent was at Ermenonville. There were also *fermes ornées* at Château du Raincy (in Seine-Saint-Denis) and Chantilly. It was the latter that provided the model for Marie Antoinette's *hameau* in the Petit Trianon.

A *fabrique* is a decorative garden building or ornamental feature. Some take the form of ruins, such as the ruined column (accommodating a house) at the Désert de Retz. Others are buildings adopted from other cultures, such as Chinese pagodas, Egyptian pyramids, and Turkish tents. The *fabriques* in the garden at Monceau (close to the Arc de Triomphe in Paris) include a pyramid, a Chinese pavilion, a windmill, and a classical colonnade. Similarly, at Château de Bagatelle (in the Bois de Boulogne), the *fabriques* included a pagoda, a windmill, a hermitage, a Swiss cottage, a Turkish tent, an obelisk, and an assortment of ruins.

The French landscape garden that emerged in the 18th century is variously known as the *jardin anglais*, *jardin à l'anglaise*, the *jardin paysager*, and the *jardin pittoresque*. These terms are not necessarily conterminous, but rather indicate different perspectives on the landscape garden that in considerable measure supplanted the formal *jardin à la française* represented by Le Nôtre: *à l'anglaise* acknowledges origins in the English landscape garden, *paysager* gestures towards the centrality of an idealized landscape, and *pittoresque* emphasizes debts to the paintings of Claude Lorrain and Nicolas Poussin.

The most influential French landscape garden of the 18th century was Ermenonville, the estate of the Marquis de Girardin, laid out from 1765 to 1776 near Senlis (Oise). The area to the east of the château represented fertility, and was laid out as a *ferme ornée*. By contrast, the Désert on the west side was a calculatedly wild and rocky landscape that represented untamed nature. The view to the south, over a man-made lake, was conceived as an Arcadian landscape evocative of the paintings of Claude Lorrain. The view to the north was meant to evoke northern landscapes, and so the *fabriques* included a windmill, a watermill, and a Dutch brewery.

The two principal influences on Ermenonville were a novel by Jean-Jacques Rousseau and the English garden known as The Leasowes. At one point in Rousseau's *Julie, ou la nouvelle Héloïse* (1761), the heroine, Julie, entertains her former lover in the garden that she has created. This Elysée, as the garden is called, formed the basis of one section of the picturesque garden of Ermenonville. The debts to *La Nouvelle Héloïse* include the Rustic Temple, the Monument to Old Loves, the Tower of Clarence, and the grove known as the Bocage. In 1778 Rousseau accepted an invitation to live at Ermenonville, where he was accommodated in a rubble-built thatched cabin with a view of the lake. He died at Ermenonville six weeks later; one hopes that the inadequacy of the cabin was not a contributory factor. The other influence was The Leasowes, the estate of the poet William Shenstone, in the English Midlands. This garden, which will be discussed in the chapter on Britain, had many features that were imitated at Ermenonville, so there were memorials to poets (including one to Shenstone), classical ruins, and temples. There was also a *ferme ornée* at Ermenonville, but its buildings no longer exist.

The 19th and 20th centuries

The French Revolution inaugurated a period of instability that was to last for more than half a century. The overthrow of the *ancien régime* shifted power from the aristocracy to the state, and the decline of aristocratic patronage inevitably had an effect on large gardens. The *jardin anglais* had the advantage of low-maintenance lawns rather than high-maintenance flower beds, so many parterres were grassed over, and trees left untrimmed. The stability of the Third Republic (instituted in 1870) heralded a return of the flower bed (sometimes with a single species, and sometimes with English carpet bedding) and a revival of the *jardin à la française*. This period also saw the advent of plant collectors' gardens, a fashion given imperial approval by Empress Joséphine's Malmaison. Many notable collectors' gardens concentrated on trees. The finest examples include the arboretum at Maison de Chateaubriand (Hauts de Seine) and Philippe André de Vilmorin's arboretum, which is now the Arboretum national des Barres (Loiret).

The best known of the private gardens of the late 19th century is Claude Monet's garden at Giverny (Eure), which was restored in the 1980s. The part of the garden near the house is laid out in long profusely planted flower beds separated by gravel paths. On the other side of what is now a railway line, Monet established a water garden centred on a pond filled with the water lilies that he loved to paint (see Figure 11). He also repeatedly painted views of the water garden that included the Japanese bridge, which must now be the most photographed of all garden bridges. Indeed, part of the power of the garden for visitors is that it is an inversion of the picturesque garden: it was not designed to resemble a picture, but rather evokes recollections of Monet's many paintings of the garden.

11. Claude Monet, *Water Lilies and Japanese Bridge*, 1899.

The most important French modernist designer of the early 20th century was Jean-Claude Nicolas Forestier, whose work in Paris includes the rose garden at Château de Bagatelle (in the Bois de Boulogne) and, together with two colleagues, the gardens of the Champ-de-Mars leading up to the Eiffel Tower. The axial layout of the Champ-de-Mars gardens recalls the great French classical gardens, and also positions the Eiffel Tower as the world's most prominent garden eye-catcher.

Twentieth-century France was the artistic capital of the Western world, but surprisingly few artistic movements had an impact on garden art. There is, however, one well-known cubist garden, the Villa Noailles (now the Hyeres Parc St Bernard), on the French Riviera. The garden was designed by the Armenian architect Gabriel Guevrekian, whose previous work included the Jardin d'Eau et de Lumière, a triangular garden (divided into smaller triangles) that he had built for the 1925 Exposition internationale des arts décoratifs et industriels modernes. The triangular motif was replicated at Villa Noailles, where the triangular garden protrudes from the house like the bow of a ship.

Many of France's finest 20th-century gardens have been historic recreations, of which the most remarkable may be the garden of the Château de Villandry, near the River Cher, in the Loire Valley. The château's original 16th-century gardens were lost under a *jardin anglais*, but an early 20th-century owner, Joachim Carvallo, created new Renaissance gardens, including an ornamental garden, a water garden, a maze, and an ornamental kitchen garden (*potager décoratif*). It is the potager that is the garden's most famous feature (see Figure 12). Each of the potager's nine squares is subdivided into geometrical beds edged with box, and within the box two seasonal crops of vegetables are grown. The planting is organized with a view to achieving sharply contrasting colours. The result is what is arguably the world's most compelling vegetable patch.

12. The Potager, Château de Villandry.

In recent decades the best known of France's landscape designers include Alain Provost and Gilles Clément. Provost has created important gardens in Paris, including the Parc Floral in the Bois de Vincennes and the Jardin Diderot at La Défence; beyond Paris, he was also the landscape architect of Eurotunnel. The designs of Gilles Clément are informed by environmentalist considerations and by an enthusiasm for waste and fallow land (*friche*) that is colonized by a variety of plants, resulting in what he calls a 'movement garden' (*jardin en mouvement*) that is part of a global 'third landscape' (*tier-paysage*) left to evolve naturally. Clément and Provost worked together on the Parc André Citroën, a modernist park in Paris built on the site of an abandoned car and armaments factory. Features in the garden include a vast lawn, two greenhouses, a canal, six colour-themed 'serial gardens', and a *jardin en mouvement*. Since 1999 it has been possible for visitors to view the garden from a tethered balloon, and so to achieve an overview that would have been the envy of generations of French garden designers.

Chapter 6
Spain and Portugal

Spain

The two greatest gardens of the Spanish Golden Age were commissioned by King Philip II at Aranjuez and the Escorial. The 14th-century palace at Aranjuez (south of Madrid) passed to the Spanish crown in 1522. The Emperor Charles V (Carlos I of Spain) built a hunting lodge on the site, and this was enlarged by Philip II, who planted the English elms that render the landscape so distinctive. The gardens that Philip II laid out in the early 1560s showed the influence of both Flemish and Italian gardens. The chief Flemish element was the use of small compartments with clipped hedges; the Italian influence is apparent in the large statues of mythological figures. This garden contained many fountains, some with stacked basins; some of the fountains now in the garden may date from this early garden. In the 1580s Philip decided to incorporate a nearby island in the Tagus into the garden that is now known as the Jardín de la Isla. This garden, which is bounded by the canal (La Ría) on one side and the river on the other sides, was laid out with avenues of plane trees. In the 18th century parterres and avenues of lime trees were planted, but elements of the Renaissance gardens can still be seen.

The gardens of the Escorial were laid out by the architect Juan de Herrara and the gardener Marcos de Cordona. The gardens outside the palace are not well documented (apart from a hanging garden described by early travellers), but the original terraces on which the gardens were built have survived. Inside the palace there are gardens in the courtyards; the finest of the courtyards is the vast Court of the Evangelists (Patio de los Evangelistas), which has at its centre an octagonal temple surrounded by four square pools fed by small fountains built into the statues of the evangelists.

In the early 17th century the garden of Buen Retiro was laid out for King Philip IV on the eastern edge of Madrid. The designer was the Florentine Cosimo Lotti, who began work in 1628 and later went on to contribute to the development of the gardens of Aranjuez. Behind the palace, Lotti established an area known as the Octagón, a star-shaped set of eight *allées* that pierced the woodland around the palace; each *allée* was bordered by fruit trees and flowers supported on trellises. Canals converging on a large octagonal pool were furnished with ornamental boats (including gondolas) that could be used in the grand entertainments mounted by the king. The garden was also the setting for meetings of literary academies, and in the mid-17th century accommodated at least seven hermits; these genuine hermits were the predecessors of the ornamental hermits of 18th-century English gardens. The surviving gardens are now a public park.

The grand *jardin à la française* inaugurated by André Le Nôtre and embodied in Versailles became a model for large gardens throughout Europe. The finest example of the style in Spain is the garden of La Granja de San Ildefonso, in Segovia, on which work began in 1720. La Granja was initiated by Philip V of Spain, who was the son of the French *dauphin*, the grandson of Louis XIV, and the first Bourbon king of Spain. King Philip was born and raised at Versailles, and commissioned a French architect, French royal gardeners, and French sculptors to build the garden. There are naturally many features in common with Versailles—an axial layout, parterres, bosquets, pools, fountains, etc.—but in the past there was one important difference that is no longer apparent: the greater contrasts in elevation at La Granja meant that the fountains were much more powerful than those at Versailles (until the latter were converted to electric power), and the vast cascade at La Granja (with a fall of more than fifty metres) is unmatched at Versailles.

In the late 18th century, the neoclassical style was represented by El Laberinto de Horta, in a suburb of Barcelona, and the picturesque style by El Capricho de la Alameda de Osuna, on th edge of Madrid. The Laberinto de Horta (now known by its Catalan name, Parc del Laberint d'Horta) is named after its principal feature, a large maze on the lowest of the three terraces, consisting of 750 metres of trimmed cypress. The middle terrace has Italianate pavilions (the architect of the garden was the Italian Domenica Bagutti), 'Roman' temples, and a grand staircase leading to the top terrace, which is centred on a pavilion (dedicated to the nine muses) overlooking a large pond. The name of El Capricho de la Alameda ('the caprice of the avenue') gestures towards the element of whimsy expressed within a structured setting. The area closest to the house of the Duchess of Osuna was a formal garden, but most of the land was given over to a *jardín inglés* with winding paths, a lake, and follies including a grotto and a hermitage.

The blending of traditions in El Capricho became characteristic of the great gardens of 19th-century Spain. The Jardines de Narváez in Andalucia, for example, has an overall design that reflects the French classical tradition, but the planting is informally Romantic and use of water recalls Islamic traditions. Similarly, the Carmen de los Mártires, on the southern slope of the Alhambra hill in Granada, is a sumptuous mid-19th-century garden that in its recently restored form incorporates formal French features, an English landscape garden, a kitchen garden, a picturesque lake in the Romantic tradition, and an Islamic colonnade.

In the early 20th century Spanish architecture was revolutionized by the Catalan architect Antoni Gaudí, whose best known garden is Parc Güell, built between 1900 and 1914 in Barcelona. The park was originally conceived as a garden suburb, but only two houses were ever built. In keeping with the ideals of the Catalan Renaixença that had emerged from a broader modernist movement, Gaudí sought to structure the landscape (on a steep slope at the edge of the city) on forms that derived from nature. The retaining walls, for example, resemble the trunks of the trees planted on top of them (see Figure 13). The ideology of the park is worn lightly, so the ambience is playful rather than solemn. The element of surprise is best embodied in the main entrance, which is situated between two surreal entrance lodges. The visitor proceeds up a staircase within which Gaudí placed a brightly coloured mosaic salamander. The principal terrace is encompassed by a long bench-balustrade in the shape of a serpent, decorated with bright mosaics in abstract patterns. The visual effect is enhanced by birdsong, a product of Gaudí's decision to embed hundreds of birds' nests within his structures; parrots that have colonized the area add to the vibrancy of colour. Planting mostly takes the form of trees, as Gaudí sought to create a forest above the city.

13. **Park Güell, Barcelona.**

Elsewhere in Spain, the most important garden designer of the early 20th century was the French designer Jean-Claude Nicolas Forestier, whose designs in Spain include the Parque de María Luisa in Seville (1911; a Moorish paradise garden), the Parc Laribal in Barcelona (1916; contains an imitation of the Patio de la Acequia in the Generalife in Granada), and his finest private garden, La Casa del Rey Moro (House of the Moorish King) in Ronda (1912), which is laid out on a steep terrace above the river. The winding staircase that descends to the river takes the visitor through a long sequence of small gardens in which views change constantly.

The most influential Spanish garden designer of the late 20th and early 21st century is Fernando Caruncho, who has heralded (and perhaps caused) the revival of the designer private garden in Spain. His gardens are at once contemporary in their principled minimalism and historicized in their recollections of the Moorish gardens of Andalucia. In one respect his gardens are an antidote to Gaudí, in that he eschews bright colours (in flowers as well as decoration) in favour of constructions emphasizing the structured use of natural light. Caruncho's best known garden is the Mas de les Voltes. which he designed in 1997 in Castell d'Empordá, in Catalonia; its central feature is a series of rectangular parterres planted entirely in wheat; the parterres are separated by *allées* lined by cypresses and olive trees.

Portugal

Portuguese gardens of the 16th and 17th centuries incorporated features that can be traced to the Roman occupation (tessellated tiles), the Moorish occupation (notably the Arabic water tank, an architectural pool of still water), and the Spanish occupation of the late 16th and early 17th centuries (especially the glazed tiles known as *azulejos*), but the design elements came from France (box parterres and pleached trees) and Italy (fountains, grottoes, statues, and *giardini segreti*). The hilly terrain occasioned a natural preference for the Italian terrace rather than the flatter French garden.

The combination of *azulejos* and water tanks was uniquely Portuguese. Arab architecture had traditionally used still water to reflect clouds and trees. The Portuguese water tank achieves a similar effect by setting *azulejos* above the stone sides of the water tank, so that the water is reflected in the shimmering blues, purples, yellows, greens, and oranges of the *azulejos*. And just as rich surface decoration in mosaic is an important element in Islamic architecture, so the constructed elements in Portuguese gardens (pavilions, fountains, grottoes, loggias) were covered in *azulejos*. The important difference between these traditions, however, is that Sunni Islamic decoration is geometrical, whereas from the mid-15th century Portuguese *azulejos* were representational, depicting plants, animals, and humans; they were used, like frescoes in Italy, to illustrate classical and biblical legends.

The best surviving Golden Age gardens in Portugal are the Quinta da Bacalhoa (Estremadura) and Castelo Branco (Beira Baixa). The villa at Bacalhoa, which was built in 1480, was acquired in 1528 by Afonso de Albuquerque, the son (and namesake) of the Portuguese admiral. The garden is a square bounded on two sides by the house and on a third side by a clipped hedge. This is an open Renaissance garden rather than an enclosed medieval garden, so the fourth side is unbounded. The garden was meant to be viewed from the arcaded loggia on the first floor of the house, and the absence of a barrier on the fourth side facilitates a view of the orchards and open countryside beyond the garden.

In 1598 the Bishop of Guarda built a palace and laid out a terraced garden in Castelo Branco, a hill town in the Serra da Estrela. On the highest terrace there is an oblong water tank surrounded by a stone balustrade; at one end a flight of steps leads down to the water. The tank was once decorated with masks and pebble mosaics and *azulejos*, most of which have disappeared, but even in its denuded state the tank is very beautiful. On the terraces below there are twin staircases lined with statues of kings on the balustrades. There is also a pond garden, through the surface of which protrude marble flower beds; the effect of brightly coloured flowers apparently growing out of the water derives ultimately from Mughal gardens, and was probably transmitted to Portugal through Moorish influence (see Figure 14).

In 1640 Fernando Mascarenhas commanded the army that succeeded in liberating Portugal from sixty years of Spanish rule. In 1671, his newly ennobled son, João de Mascarenhas, Marquês de Fronteira, commissioned a garden for the Palácio dos Marquês de Fronteira, which he was building near Lisbon. This garden, which includes a vast parterre of clipped box with occasional gaps for roses, culminates in a huge water tank in front of a large arcaded wall; the arches of the wall are decorated with brightly coloured *azulejos* depicting military scenes. The low walls on the sides of the terracing are also decorated with pictorial *azulejos* depicting a variety of mythological and patriotic scenes.

The early 18th-century Bom Jesus do Monto (Good Jesus of the Hill), near Braga, in northern Portugal, could justly be described as a staircase with a garden. The church is a pilgrimage site, and is reached by a monumental baroque stairway that rises 115 metres (380 feet). The staircase zigzags up the steep hill through a series of highly ornamented landings, each of which has a fountain, a floor decorated with mosaics, and walls surmounted with topiary. The staircase represents spiritual ascent, and its decoration is organized in a devotional programme; pilgrims proceeding up the stairs on their knees may pause by biblical quotations and depictions of biblical scenes.

The grandest garden of 18th-century Portugal is the garden of the Palácio Nacional de Queluz, near Lisbon. The two principal formal gardens of the palace, the Jardim Pênsil (Garden of

14. The pond garden, Episcopal Palace, Castelo Branco.

Neptune; 1762) and the Jardim Malta (Garden of Malta; 1764),
were both designed by the French architect Jean-Baptiste Robill,
who spent much of his career in Portugal (where he is known as
Joâo Baptista Robillon). The Garden of Neptune, which is laid out
above a large water tank, consists mostly of clipped box arranged
in patterns that resemble mazes; the pools in this garden are
decorated with statues carved in stone or moulded in lead. The
principal feature of the Garden of Malta, so called because the
future King Pedro III was Grand Master of the Knights of Malta,
is an elegant sunken parterre with a scalloped pool at its centre,
from which paths edged with box (sometimes in topiary) radiate.
In addition to these formal gardens, the palace also has on its
south side a woodland arranged around an axial walkway (with
intersecting *allées*) culminating in a vast cascade. To the north-west
of the palace there is an ornamental boating canal, the sides of
which are decorated with *azulejos*.

The prevailing idiom of the gardens of 19th-century Portugal
was that of the picturesque Romantic tradition. Two of the best
examples were established in the Sintra Hills near Lisbon. In 1789
an Englishman called Gerard de Visme built a Gothic house at
Monserrate, and six years later rented it to the Gothic novelist
William Beckford, who had fled to Portugal after a scandal.
Beckford strove to create a Romantic garden by erecting follies,
including a Gothic pavilion and a waterfall; he also imported a flock
of sheep from his English estate, Fonthill Abbey. In 1856 Monserrate
was bought by Francis Cook (later Visconde de Monserrate), who
remodelled the house and planted vast numbers of subtropical
plants. The garden eventually became derelict, but both house
and garden have been restored, and are open to the public.

The Pena Palace, built by Ferdinand II (the king-consort) on a
rocky site near Monserrate in 1829, is a Gothic palace around
which Ferdinand created a large park in which he accentuated the
ruggedness of the landscape with streams and lakes, built follies,
and chose plants designed to create a luxuriant atmosphere, such

as camellias, rhododendrons, and tree ferns. The overall effect is sometimes described as Wagnerian; indeed, Richard Strauss famously declared Pena to be the garden of Klingsor in the second act of *Parsifal*.

In 20th-century Portugal, the most creative period for garden design was the 1930s. The most accomplished garden of the period is the Parque de Serralves, the modernist garden in Oporto designed in 1932 by the French landscape architect and urban planner Jacques Gréber. The garden of Serralves has the long axial structure of classical French design, and the art deco villa is central to the design. The long descent from the Casa de Serralves to a lake is a water garden replete with cascades and fountains and pools, lined with ivy and decorated with topiary. The surrounding park has avenues of horse chestnut and sweetgum. It is one of the world's greatest modernist gardens, and its basis in a European movement is a reminder that the richness of Portuguese gardens has always been enhanced by the welcoming of traditions from the wider world.

Chapter 7
Northern Europe

The Low Countries

The Renaissance in the Low Countries had a markedly different character from the Renaissance in Italy, and garden art is one of the forms in which the differences are readily apparent. There was certainly Italian influence on design, but there were two other important factors. First, there was a strong element of continuity with the medieval Netherlandish garden, which bequeathed to later gardens the idea of outdoor rooms variously containing ornamental and fragrant flowers, pavilions with statues, lakes, orchards, vineyards, and menageries; some of these elements survive at Het Binnenhof in The Hague and at Rosendael in Gelderland. Second, the piety that is a distinctive feature of the Dutch Renaissance is responsible for Christian images in Dutch gardens. This is a marked contrast to the paganism typical of Italian gardens which prompted the remark attributed to Queen Christina of Sweden, on seeing the gardens of the Villa Farnese, that 'I dare not speak the name of Jesus lest I break the spell'.

A strong sense of this spirituality pervades the ideal and emblematical garden of Erasmus's *Convivium religiosum* (*The Godly Feast*, 1522). Erasmus proclaims the protector of his imaginary garden to be Jesus rather than Priapus (a classical god of fertility), and at the entrance visitors encounter the fountain of St Peter rather than pagan monsters. His square garden is bounded on three sides by a pillared gallery accommodating a library and an aviary. The garden is divided by a brook which drains a fountain and flows into a decorated stucco basin; the purpose of the water is to refresh and cleanse the soul. The ornamental and fragrant plants are laid out in beds, and each species is labelled with its name and virtues.

All the elements of this godly garden were present in Dutch gardens of the 16th century. The gardens of Jan Vredeman de Vries, the most influential designer of the century, contained medieval and Erasmian elements laid out with a painterly attention to detail and form. The most important architectural element in his gardens was the Erasmian gallery, which overlooked complementary structures containing fountains and parterres. The intricate parterres of Dutch gardens included a much higher proportion of rare foreign plants than did gardens elsewhere. This predilection for the exotic was encouraged by the establishment in Leiden of what was to become Europe's most important botanical garden, and facilitated by the voyages of the Dutch fleet to Asia.

The truce that ended the Revolt of the Netherlands in 1609 proved to mark a permanent division between the Netherlands (the United Provinces) and the Spanish Netherlands (now Belgium), and thereafter population movements accentuated the cultural divisions between the Protestant north and the Catholic south. The republicanism of the north drew on the ideals of the ancient Roman republic; one cultural manifestation arising from this ideology was the classicizing impulse in 17th-century architecture, including garden architecture. The earliest important example of this style was Honselaarsdijk, the estate of Prince Frederik Hendrik, between The Hague and the Hook of Holland. This was the first large garden in northern Europe to be designed on Albertian principles of harmonic ratios; it also inaugurated the Dutch tradition of the tree-lined canal garden.

The Flemish gardens of the 15th and 16th centuries inevitably had much in common with Dutch gardens, but Spanish influence was always more pronounced in the southern Netherlands than in the northern provinces, and Italian influence on garden design became more pronounced in the late 16th century. Gardens in this period tended to be flat, not so much because of French influence, but rather because the terraces of Italian gardens could only be achieved if the land was already hilly and if gardens were being constructed on a grand scale; neither was the case in the southern Netherlands. The other difference between Italian and Flemish gardens in this period is that, although there were fountains, water played a relatively small part in Flemish gardens, whereas it was the central feature of many of the great Italian gardens.

A continued medieval influence manifested itself in a tendency to enclose gardens with walls and hedges. Gardens were laid out in parterres, and the geometrical intricacy of the patterns of planting became the most characteristic feature of Flemish design. The shrubs planted in the parterres were pruned into geometrical shapes, and were laid out in regular patterns; individual parterres were typically enclosed with palisades.

Architectural features tended to be restricted to fountains and statues. Instead of the stone loggias of Italian gardens, Flemish designers favoured outdoor rooms walled entirely by clipped hedges, often supported on wooden frames. Sometimes even the expected statue at the centre of the parterre was replaced by a bare-trunked tree with sculpted foliage. The introduction of exotic plants was encouraged by the publications of the Flemish botanist Julius Dodoens. There was particular enthusiasm for the tulip and the lily, but collectors' gardens, such as the one established in Borgerhout (near Antwerp) in about 1550, built up collections of hundreds of foreign plants.

The most important botanical garden of the late 16th century was in Leiden. The Hortus Academicus at Leiden was founded by the

University of Leiden in 1587, but planting did not begin until 1594. The delay was caused in part by the difficulty in securing the appointment of Carolus Clusius, the greatest living botanist, as the founding curator of the garden. The garden was used for teaching, but also became the main European centre for the collection and dissemination of plants from around the world. Most of the world's cultivated geraniums (*Pelargonium*) and evening primroses (*Oenothera*) originate in this garden, which also bequeathed the tulip to the world. The garden is still used for research by the university's botanists. The original design was submerged in a new planting plan devised in 1730 (in part by Linnaeus), but the original layout and planting of Clusius and his head gardener, Clutius (Dirck Outgaerzoon Cluyts), were replicated in a new garden built in 1931 across the canal from the original garden.

There was French influence during this period, particularly in the introduction of *parterres de broderie* by André Mollet. After the revocation of the Treaty of Nantes in 1685, French Huguenot designers sought refuge in the Netherlands, and French influence increased. Daniel Marot, who was among the refugees, was appointed as an interior designer and landscape architect by Willem III (later William III of England, Scotland, and Ireland), and so brought the baroque style associated with the court of Louis XIV to the Netherlands. The royal garden at Het Loo (Apeldoorn) was enlarged and adapted to French models, with a central axis running through the palace and discrete parts of the garden being subsumed in unified designs, with *parterres de broderie* centred on fountains and pools. Het Loo was extended in 1692 on a scale that made it rival Versailles—but with better waterworks. The gardens were obliterated by King Louis Napoleon (younger brother of the Emperor), but imaginatively restored in 1984 to the design of 1684.

The 18th-century style known as the Dutch Régence does not (despite the French form) refer to the minority of Louis XV of France, but rather to the rule of the Netherlands by the 'regents' (*regenten*), which were prominent burgher families. In the early part of the century the gardens of the *regenten* were miniature versions of Willem III's gardens, and closely followed courtly fashion in their immaculately groomed hedges and complex parterres, in garden buildings such as orangeries and tea houses, and in collections of exotic plants.

Towards the middle of the century, styles became more informal as English and Dutch taste gradually converged. In the second half of the century the English landscape garden began to appear, initially by way of German landscape designers, notably Johann Georg Michael, who was known as a 'woodland gardener' (*boschgardenier*). Michael created landscape gardens near Haarlem (Beeckestijn, Velserbeek, and Haarlemmerhout) and in Gelderland (Kasteel Biljoen, Kasteel Doorwerth, and Kasteel Staverden); all survive, albeit in modified form. Michael employed Jan David Zocher, a German gardener who subsequently married his daughter. The Zocher dynasty was to remain an important presence in Dutch landscape design until World War I. Their most famous creation is the Keukenhof Garden, designed by the Zochers in 1857 and transformed in 1950 into a permanent exhibition of spring-flowering bulbs. Keukenhof now has a global reputation, and its proprietors proudly declare it to be the most beautiful spring garden in the world. It would be difficult to think of a rival candidate.

The landscape garden was the prevailing Dutch idiom until the early 20th century, when the influence of the Arts and Crafts movement began to be felt in cottage-style gardens. In recent decades several of the most influential designers have been members of West 8, the landscape architecture company founded in 1987 by Adriaan Geuze, whose gardens around the world aspire to integrate urban identity, contemporary culture, and public space. The Central Waterfront in Toronto, for example, attempts to mediate between the city and the lake with a sustainable and ecologically responsible 'green foot' organized along a promenade.

Dutch designers also lie at the heart of the global New Perennial Movement (inspired by the wild gardens of William Robinson, on whom see the chapter on Britain), which seeks to accommodate 'wild nature' into designs by concentrating on the form and structure of plants rather than their colour. The principal figures in the movement are Piet Oudolf, whose best known recent work is the planting of the New High Line Park on a former elevated railway in New York City, and Mien Ruys, whose legacy is maintained in the Tuinen Mien Ruys, a sequence of thirty naturalistic gardens in Dedemsvaart, a small town in the eastern Netherlands.

Germany

The Renaissance garden in Germany is confined to the few years between 1590 and the outbreak of the Thirty Years War in 1618. It was stimulated during this period both by travellers who had seen the gardens of Italy and by the translation into German of French and Italian books on gardening.

Many German Renaissance gardens, including four important Italianate gardens in Munich, are known only from the descriptions provided by Philipp Hainhofer in his *Reise-Tagebuch* (travel diary) of 1612. Only one Renaissance garden within what is now Germany is fully documented, and that is the Hortus Palatinus, in the grounds of Heidelberg Castle. The designer was the Huguenot Salomon de Caus, who worked for the royal family in England and then followed Princess Elizabeth to Heidelberg after her marriage to the Elector in 1613. The gardens, on which work began in 1615, are constructed on five narrow terraces with high retaining walls. The terraces were divided into compartments by hedges and pergolas, and are decorated with a maze, statues, gazebos, and ornamental ponds. These characteristic features are supplemented by waterworks and grottoes with automata, including water organs for which Caus composed the music. The terraces and a grotto remain today, but the planting is modern and Caus's buildings are in ruins.

Garden art was slow to recover after the conclusion of the Thirty Years War in 1648. By the time that new gardens were being commissioned, the favoured style was baroque, the principal model was Versailles, and many of the designers were French. At Herrenhausen, near Hanover, the first pleasure garden, laid out in 1666, recalled the design of Renaissance Italian villas. In the 1670s a French designer (Henri Perronet) began to develop the garden, notably by the addition of fountains.

The most celebrated period in the garden's history was the 1680s, when Sophia of Hanover (later the Electress) commissioned the Großer Garten (Great Garden). Her designer was Martin Charbonnier, a pupil of André Le Nôtre. Countess Sophia had grown up in the Dutch Republic, where her family had found refuge during the Thirty Years War. She accordingly dispatched Charbonnier to the Netherlands to study garden design. The origins of the garden in an Italianate design, together with Charbonnier's French background and Dutch studies, led to the creation of a syncretic baroque garden that combines Italian, French, and Dutch elements. In 1692 Countess Sophia extended the garden to its present capacious size. The garden is rectangular, and bordered by a tree-lined canal. The layout around a central axis is rigorously geometrical. Beyond the central parterre there are two garden rooms: a theatre and a maze. The hedge theatre is still in use for theatrical and musical productions. The central fountain, created in the early 18th century, propelled water to a height of thirty-five metres (it is now electrified, and reaches twice that height). The garden was originally designed around the Schloss, which was destroyed by British bombs in 1943. After the war the ruins were removed, and for more than sixty years the effect of the garden was diminished by the absence of the Schloss. Happily, the Schloss has now been rebuilt, and what is now the Herrenhausen Palace Museum opened in 2013.

The last of the classical French garden designers in Germany was Dominique Girard, who, like Charbonnier, had trained under

André Le Nôtre. Louis XIV arranged for Girard to work for the deposed Elector of Bavaria, Maximilian II Emanuel, who was living in exile at Château de Saint-Cloud. Like Sophia of Hanover, Maximilian had lived in the Netherlands (as Governor of the Spanish Netherlands), and the gardens that he built had Dutch canals, lined with trees. When Maximilian was restored in 1701, he took Girard with him to Munich, where Girard worked with Charles Carbonet (another pupil of Le Nôtre) on Schloss Nymphenburg and Schloss Schleißheim.

At Schloss Nymphenburg, Girard (following Carbonet) created a large French baroque garden with a long axial canal. In the 19th century this garden was largely overlaid by an English landscape garden, but French features such as the parterre and the principal canal have survived. At Schloss Schleißheim, a palace complex north of Munich, Girard retained the existing network of canals, but installed a large parterre in front of the palace. This baroque garden became derelict in the early 19th century, but was never overbuilt, and was ably restored in the 1860s.

In the first half of the 18th century, as baroque yielded to rococo, grandeur in garden design was displaced by elegance, playfulness, and a taste for *chinoiserie* and labyrinthine shapes. There are many fine German examples, such as Frederick II's Sanssouci (1745) at Potsdam, the whimsical gardens of his sister the Margravine Wilhelmina in Bayreuth (the Hermitage, *c.*1735, and Sanspareil, *c.*1745), and Prince Heinrich of Prussia's Rheinsberg, in Brandenburg (started 1744).

The best preserved German rococo garden is Veitshöchheim, the summer residence of the Prince-Bishops of Würzburg, in Bavaria. In 1702 the garden was walled and the formal structures were established. After the hiatus of the Seven Years War (1754–63) the garden was remodelled in a sumptuous rococo style by Prince-Bishop Adam Friedrich von Seinsheim. The garden is divided into many rooms defined by hedges, and the architectural features include a grotto beneath a 'Snail House' (Schneckenhaus, a small house covered in shells) and two vaguely oriental pavilions with roofs embellished with pineapples. There are also two lakes, the larger of which has a Mount Parnassus with a statue of Pegasus rising from its summit.

In the second half of the 18th century the rococo garden in Germany was supplanted by the English landscape garden, of which the seminal example in Germany was Wörlitz, the estate of Prince Franz von Anhalt-Dessau. Prince Franz was an Enlightenment intellectual whose journeys through Europe included four visits to England, where he had come to admire English agriculture (including ornamental farm buildings), horticulture, and arboriculture. In the course of forty years (1764–*c*.1804) he created a 'garden kingdom' (*Gartenreich*) that occupied some ninety square miles (*c*.150 square km). More than half of this garden kingdom survives, and is rightly designated as a UNESCO World Heritage Site on the grounds that it embodies a realization of the ideals of the Enlightenment in a designed landscape that integrates art, education, and economic viability.

Of the six parks and gardens in the complex, the most important is the Wörlitz Garden, which was the first landscape garden in Germany. This garden has five distinct sections, connected by bridges, footpaths, and ferries. Some of the garden features were unprecedented. The Palace Garden, for example, included a version of the Temple of Hercules Victor in Rome that was equipped on the inside for use as a synagogue by local Jews; this expression of Enlightenment tolerance was eventually to be despoiled during *Kristallnacht*. Similarly, the Neue Anlage (New Grounds) contains Europe's only artificial volcano, a copy of Vesuvius that has fierce eruptions of fire and lava.

The first of Germany's important public gardens was developed in the 1790s, when the Elector of Bavaria, Karl Theodor, together with his *aide-de-camp*, the Anglo-American loyalist exile

Benjamin Thompson, devised a plan to lay out an English garden in Munich for the benefit of the general public. Friedrich Ludwig von Sckell, who had studied landscape gardening in England, was charged with designing this *Volksgarten*, which soon became known by its present name, the Englische Garten. Thompson oversaw the construction of the garden, which included, in addition to capacious areas for the public, a military garden, an arable farm, a sheep farm, and a cattle farm with an associated veterinary school.

City parks continued to be created throughout the 19th century, notably by Gustav Meyer, who was Berlin's first Director of Gardens, and Peter Joseph Lenné, whose Berlin gardens include Pfaueninsel and the park at Charlottenburg. Both Meyer and Lenné worked all over Germany as advisers and planners. The style that they evolved as part of their wish to provide parks accessible to both middle-class citizens who wanted public spaces to affirm their standing and working-class citizens who wanted a place of refreshment led to widespread recognition of what became known as the Meyer–Lenné School of landscape design.

In the opening years of the 20th century, the Arts and Crafts garden began to gain momentum in Germany, particularly in the work of Hermann Muthesius, whose advocacy of a structural relationship between house and garden was very influential. Such civilized reflection on the nature of the garden was soon swept aside by the horrors of war, and then by the evil ideology of National Socialism. The Nazi cult of blood and soil (*Blut und Boden*) had a horticultural dimension, in that it emphasized not only ancestry, but also the bond of Aryan people to the land that they cultivate. This rural fantasy was taken up by garden designers, notably Willy Lange, who spurned the structured garden in favour of natural patterns rooted in the soil, by which he meant that plants should be arranged on biological principles appropriate to their region of origin.

In the post-war years a divided Germany produced different sorts of gardens. In East Germany, the Soviet Park of Culture and Rest was replicated in the Kulturpark. In the West, many historic gardens were restored (notably the Tiergarten in West Berlin), and new gardens often had a historical component. The burgeoning of apartment blocks on both sides of the city reduced spaces in poorer areas, and the designed green areas (disparagingly known as *Abstandsgrün*, green spacing) between buildings was seldom treated imaginatively. In recent decades, however, these strips have often been appropriated for community gardens.

In 1989 the Berlin Wall came down, and within a few days Berliners began to plant trees and shrubs on the death strip. The soil had been rendered toxic by weedkillers (to ensure a clear line of fire), so these early plantings were not destined to prosper. The civic authorities took note of this spontaneous attempt to create a garden, and commissioned Gustav Lange to design the Mauerpark ('wall park'), a linear park built on the site of a section of the Wall. A thirty-metre section of the Wall has been preserved in the park, and is constantly repainted by graffiti artists. It is an immensely active place, with bands in the summer, a weekly flea market, karaoke, *boules* competitions, and a lively and mildly disreputable night life. The site of the death strip of poisoned land, heavy with the memory of state-sponsored murder, is now a garden that affirms life, a powerful symbol of a new Germany and a reunited Europe.

Russia

The origins of the garden in Russia are unknown. Moscow's gardens are documented from the late 15th century, and in the 16th century Ivan IV ('the Terrible') had formal gardens in many estates, notably Kolomenskoye, in what is now a south-east suburb of Moscow. In the 17th century, the Romanov estates included Izmaylovo, in an eastern suburb of Moscow.

Both Kolomenskoye and Izmaylovo are known to have had some Renaissance features. They are now open-air museums, but although some of the original buildings survive (and other early buildings have been added), the contours of the gardens are nowhere apparent.

In the early 18th century, Peter the Great's ambition to turn Russia into a European state had a horticultural dimension, and his own enthusiasms were shaped by the parks and gardens that he visited on his European travels. In 1697, on his first journey to Europe, Peter visited England, the Netherlands, and Austria. In England he lived for four months in the home of John Evelyn, where he and his loutish companions trashed the house and wrecked Evelyn's beloved holly hedges. In the Netherlands he was a more appreciative visitor, and on his return to Russia built his first summer palace, in St Petersburg. Both the palace and the Summer Garden, as it is now known, have Dutch features that reflect Peter's travels as well as French baroque features that reflect his reading. Paths in the Summer Garden were lined with trees trimmed to create green walls, and there was extensive topiary. There were also fountains and statues imported from Europe, many of which still survive in what is now a public park.

Eighteen years later Peter returned to Europe, this time to the Netherlands and France, and he was able to visit both Marly, where he admired the grand cascade, and Versailles, where he sailed on the Grand Canal and explored the garden. He returned to Russia determined to create something similar, and did so at his new summer palace, which is now known as Peterhof. This estate, which is understandably promoted as the Russian Versailles, was built on the Gulf of Finland. The palace stands on a terrace, and a grand cascade modelled on Marly leads down to the lower garden and the sea. The water pours down marble steps flanked by fountains into a basin ringed by statues whose centrepiece is the Samson Fountain; water rises from the open jaws of the lion more than sixty feet (twenty metres) into the air.

It is as fine a centrepiece as can be found in any of the world's gardens. The garden below the cascade is thoroughly French, with *allées*, bosquets, *jeux d'eau*, and three small palaces, each with a garden.

In the mid-18th century, the Empress Elizabeth inherited the house and garden built by her mother Catherine I (and so called Yekaterinsky) at Tsarskoye Selo, and promptly recast the estate in a grand manner that reflected both French and Italian influences: there were French *allées* and a canal, and Italian garden buildings and statues. Elizabeth was succeeded by her German nephew, Peter III, and shortly thereafter by Peter's widow, who assumed the throne as Catherine II ('the Great'). It was Catherine who introduced the English landscape garden to Russia, initially at Tsarskoye Selo. She engaged an Anglo-German designer, John Busch, and a Scottish architect, Charles Cameron, to work at Tsarskoye Selo. Cameron later went on to design both the Palladian house and the landscape garden at Pavlovsk for Catherine's son Grand Duke Paul (later Paul I). The features of Pavlovsk, which is one of the world's greatest landscape gardens, include a Palladian Temple of Friendship loosely based on the Pantheon in Rome (and a version of the design later used by Jefferson for the Rotunda at the University of Virginia), and a rustic thatched dairy that anticipated the one that Marie Antoinette was to build at her *hameau* in Versailles a few years later.

The landscape garden became the dominant form for large Russian gardens, albeit with more garden buildings than their English originals. The abolition of serfdom in 1861 deprived estate owners of cheap labour, and thereafter private estates became increasingly difficult to maintain. The Revolution of 1917 signalled the end of large private gardens, and imperial gardens were nationalized. Under the Soviets the emphasis shifted from private to state patronage, and Parks of Culture and Rest, such as Gorky Park in Moscow and the island parks of Leningrad, were built in cities all over the Soviet Union.

The construction of vast numbers of apartments for city dwellers led to a burgeoning of the dacha, and colonies of dachas, ranging from shacks to full-sized houses, were established on the edges of cities. Depending on the circumstances of the occupiers, the dacha garden was used either for the cultivation of ornamental plants or as a place to grow fruit and vegetables. In post-Soviet Russia, the wealthy 'new Russians' (*Novye Russkie*) transformed the dacha, in effect creating palaces in the countryside, and laying out eclectic gardens with extravagant fountains and statues that assert their wealth and power. In the 21st century, the quality of design has improved enormously. Designers, notably Andrei Lysikov, create imaginative dacha gardens, and Moscow's Gorky Park has since 2011 been stripped of its amusement rides and recreated as a very fine eco-friendly recreational zone.

Chapter 8
Britain

The Renaissance

The burgeoning of English gardens in the 18th and 19th centuries often obliterated earlier gardens on the same sites, so earlier English gardens are usually known only from written and pictorial documentation, or from earthworks. It is apparent from such sources that there were continuities between medieval and Renaissance gardens with respect to plants. Many of the plants that were to become important elements in Renaissance gardens had been established in the 14th century. Rosemary had been introduced in 1340, and its advent had ushered in a fashion for evergreens. Juniper, holly, box, and bay (*Laurus nobilis*) were all cultivated in early 15th-century gardens. By this time evergreens were being clipped, knot gardens (small gardens of low interlacing hedges, usually box) were being laid out in heraldic patterns, and the double-clove gillyflower (i.e. carnation) had become highly valued for its beauty and aroma.

The transition from the *hortus conclusus* of the Middle Ages to the pleasure garden of the Renaissance was effected by the Burgundian influences which began to be felt in English gardens at the end of the 15th century. The earliest large Renaissance garden was established at Henry VII's palace at Richmond (1498–1501); this garden, which did not survive the destruction of the palace in the 18th century, was laid out in enclosures linked by covered walks and galleries.

Three important gardens were built by Henry VIII at Hampton Court Palace (1531–4), Whitehall (1545), and Nonsuch Palace (1538–47). All three evinced the direct influence of French gardens in their common situation beneath the windows of the state apartments and in their common geometrical design, consisting of a square surrounded by a covered walk and divided into quarters; each quarter was laid out in knot gardens, and at the centre of each garden was a fountain. At Hampton Court Palace, the only one of these gardens to survive, there was a mount overlooking the Thames. The mount had originated in Italy (there is one in the botanical garden at Padua), but came to England through France, where Olivier de Serres had attempted to introduce it into French gardens. The canal is a late 17th-century addition inspired by Versailles.

In the second half of the 16th century, innovation in garden design shifted from the royal palaces to the houses of the aristocracy, notably Kenilworth Castle (where the garden has been recently restored to accord with its appearance in 1575), Theobalds Park, and Wimbledon House, all of which show the direct influence of French or Flemish gardens and the indirect influence of Italian gardens in their designs. One of the most ambitious designs was that of Lyveden New Bield (Northamptonshire), which included a moated garden with a raised terrace and two mounts; the garden was never finished, but its structural features still survive.

In smaller houses knot gardens became fashionable. Salomon de Caus only lived in England for a few years, but he brought with him a knowledge of Italian and French gardens (notably Pratolino, St-Germain-en-Laye, and Fontainebleau), and his incorporation of elements of these gardens in his designs for the royal gardens at Somerset House, Greenwich Palace, and Richmond Palace (all laid out between 1610 and 1612) changed the face of English design. In all three commissions he produced designs in which house and garden were conceived as integrated parts of single designs, so that the gardens were extensions of the houses.

His enthusiasm for hydraulics greatly increased the importance of water in the English garden, because the fountains, grottoes, and automata that he installed in the royal gardens quickly became features of aristocratic gardens, including Ham House (in Richmond, overlaid with a garden built in 1671, and rebuilt as a late 17th-century garden in 1975), Twickenham Park, Ware Park (Hertfordshire), Gorhambury (near St Albans), and Chastleton (Oxfordshire; both house and garden survive); hydraulics were also introduced into established gardens, such as those at Wimbledon House and Theobalds Park.

The influence of de Caus waned after his departure for Germany, but was revived by the arrival in England of his kinsman (son or brother or nephew) Isaac de Caus, who in the 1620s and early 1630s designed new gardens (all with grottoes) at the Whitehall Banqueting House, Woburn Abbey, Moor Park (Hertfordshire, now overlaid with a Capability Brown garden adapted as a golf course), and Wilton House (Wiltshire).

In 1613, when Salomon de Caus left for Germany, Inigo Jones travelled to Italy, and he returned the following year as the principal English exponent of Palladio. English gardens constructed between 1615 and 1640—Arundel House (London), Oatlands Palace (Surrey), Albury Park (Surrey; the garden was redesigned in 1677 by John Evelyn), and Danvers House (Chelsea)—were all constructed on the Palladian principles championed by Jones.

Scottish Renaissance gardens were constructed on the French model, though the hilly landscape of Scotland meant that some gardens were terraced in the Italian style, notably the lost royal garden at Linlithgow. There is little detailed documentation of Scottish gardens before the end of the 16th century, and very few gardens have survived, even in attenuated form. Falkland Palace, in Fife, had a royal gardener among its employees from 1456, but he and his successors seem to have grown little other than onions. In 1513 the wooden trellis that enclosed the garden was replaced by a stone wall, and in 1628 a plan for 'planting and contriving the garden anew' was effected, but little is known of the layout and contents, save that it included a real tennis court. The gardens are now laid out in the style of the 17th century, but this is entirely the imaginative work of the 20th-century designer Percy Cane.

The only Scottish Renaissance garden to have survived in substantially unaltered form (though not content) is the King's Knot at Stirling Castle. The garden was laid out c.1540, and was long known as the New Garden, to distinguish it from the King's Privy Garden, which was a knot garden created in 1532. There is no documentary evidence of the original plantations of the New Garden, but the surviving terraces and ramps show that this was a garden on the grand scale, laid out in a long rectangle with a central series of turf terraces rising in the form of an octagon. At the top is the King's Knot, a mount that would originally have been surmounted with a pavilion from which to view the garden.

Restoration and 18th century

In 1660, the return of the king and court from France inaugurated a period of French styles adapted to the rigours of British weather. Within a year of the Restoration, André Mollet had redesigned St James's Park in London, laying out an axial garden with a central canal and a series of avenues radiating from a central point in what the French called a *patte d'oie* (goose's foot). The most prominent exponents of this style were George London and his partner Henry Wise. Their designs included Badminton House (Gloucestershire), an axial garden with huge avenues (in which some of the original trees survive), parterres, groves, fountains, and a vast hedge maze. At Chatsworth, London and Wise diverted a river to create a grand canal, and planted *parterres de broderie*. In 1689, the accession of William and Mary to the throne introduced Dutch styles to Britain, including an emphasis on evergreens (often in topiary form) and small-scale landscape gardening.

The principal engine of the 18th-century English landscape garden was land reform: in the course of the century, some three million acres (1.2 million hectares) of common land were enclosed as private land. The availability of large tracts of land coalesced with emerging ideas about the superiority of idealized nature to patterned artifice to create the possibility of a new type of garden. The landscape garden did not supplant earlier formal styles, but rather existed alongside historic styles even after it became the dominant form. Indeed, the landscape garden often contained formal elements, as is apparent in Charles Bridgeman's design for Stowe.

Rousham (Oxfordshire) is a good example of how English gardens developed in this period. At the beginning of the 18th century, the garden still contained features inherited from its Jacobean origins, notably falling terraces centred on a series of fishponds. In the 1720s the garden was redesigned by Charles Bridgeman, who transformed the fishponds into ornamental basins and planned a garden that was broadly French in conception, with a bosquet and *allées* and paths leading to pavilions.

On Bridgeman's death in 1738 the commission passed to William Kent, and it is not clear how much of Bridgeman's design had been realized by this point. Kent refashioned the garden on broadly Italian lines, and so the much-altered fishponds were again reworked, this time with pedimented cascades, of which the uppermost was embellished by a copy of the Medici Venus.

Other Italian statues and structures followed, notably a seven-arched version of the Praeneste arcade. Kent also opened up views of the Oxfordshire landscape, in effect appropriating woodland and the agricultural landscape into the garden. As Horace Walpole memorably said of Kent, 'he leapt the fence and saw that all nature was a garden'. Kent's garden at Rousham is well preserved, and is the best surviving example of his work.

The finest example of gardens in the tradition of Bridgeman and Kent is Stourhead (Wiltshire), which was laid out between 1741 and 1772 by the proprietor, Henry Hoare the younger, and his assistant Henry Flitcroft. The garden, which is not visible from the Palladian house, is centred on a man-made lake, around which are placed classical buildings. The extent of the classicizing impulse that underlies the design of Stourhead is not fully understood, but it is certainly possible that the design was intended to use the story of Aeneas founding a nation in Virgil's *Aeneid* as a model for Hoare founding a family seat at Stourhead. The evidence for this contention includes inscriptions from the *Aeneid*, and the striking similarities between views within the garden and the pictorial representation of classical landscapes in which Aeneas figures. Such levels of associative meaning enrich a garden that is rightly celebrated for its beauty.

The notion of the associative garden that shapes the emotions and thinking of the visitor did not begin with Stourhead. Its origins lie with Alexander Pope and his garden at Twickenham. The progeny of that garden includes not only Stourhead, but also Charles Hamilton's Painshill Park (Surrey), which has been wonderfully restored in recent decades. In the 18th century the best known associative garden was William Shenstone's The Leasowes, in the English Midlands. In this garden Shenstone aspired to recreate the world of Virgil by signposting many features with quotations from Virgil and by designating part of the garden as 'Virgil's Grove', where he erected an obelisk in honour of the poet. In the gardens Shenstone built a ruined priory, temples, seats, and a cottage. There were many urns and benches, often with inscribed quotations. The arrangement of the garden features reflected an aspiration to be natural, but nonetheless conformed to the ideal of structured and melancholic contemplation of picturesque landscape. The use of inscriptions to guide the associative elements in the constructed scenery in the garden influenced the use of the same technique at Ermenonville and, in the 20th century, Little Sparta.

Alongside this tradition of the classicizing and associative garden, there was a rival landscape tradition represented by Lancelot 'Capability' Brown, who dominated English landscape design for decades. His gardens scaled down the classical element represented in buildings and statuary in favour of the creation of an idealized natural landscape, a recreated Garden of Eden in which the artifice that reshapes the landscape is invisible. His nickname, 'Capability', was not so much an affirmation of his competence as of his ability to realize the potential of a natural landscape to become an ideal landscape.

In the course of his career Capability Brown accepted more than 200 commissions, and his style became a brand: a sinuous lake created by damming a stream, an elegant bridge, clumps of trees in open landscapes and (improbably) on the summits of hills, trees marshalled around the park boundaries, and a winding entrance road affording occasional glimpses of the house. The theoretical underpinnings of his designs are unknown: the amateur classicizing designers of associative gardens were often articulate Enlightenment intellectuals, whereas Brown was a working professional who never wrote and seldom spoke about the thinking behind his gardens. Brown's serpentine curves certainly resemble the 'line of beauty' that is a central theme in William Hogarth's *The Analysis of Beauty* (1753), and the similarity may point to a common aesthetic context.

In the 1740s Brown worked at Stowe (Buckinghamshire). At the point when he began, William Kent was transforming the earlier garden designed by Charles Bridgeman, which had contained both formal French features (canals, straight avenues, and a large parterre) and pasture viewed over a ha-ha. Kent created a picturesque valley known as the Elysian Fields, and also commissioned classical buildings with inscriptions, all in the service of a complex iconography of moral and political allusions that reflected the Whiggish convictions of Lord Cobham. When Brown left Stowe to establish an independent practice in 1751, he left behind the proliferation of classical buildings, but carried on creating Elysian landscapes.

Brown's most celebrated gardens include Chatsworth (Derbyshire) and Blenheim Palace (Oxfordshire), both of which were laid out in the 1760s. The garden that he inherited (and in part dismantled) at Chatsworth had an axial layout (with parterres) designed by George London and Henry Wise, and a formal cascade by a French designer. Brown swept away both these formal elements and a nearby village, extending the park and creating a naturalistic landscape. His changes included diverting and widening the River Derwent that flowed by the house.

At Blenheim, where the formal garden had been laid out by Sir John Vanbrugh and Henry Wise, Brown retained the bridge that his predecessors had built over three canals, and created a winding lake by damming the River Glyme; the centre of the lake was narrowed to accommodate the bridge. The deference of Brown and his contemporaries to the great power of wealthy landowners came at a cost to those with no wealth and no power: their willingness to destroy villages that were inconvenient presences in their landscapes had a huge human cost for the dispossessed villagers. The practice attracted occasional criticism, notably Oliver Goldsmith's 'The Deserted Village', but such scruples did not inhibit the exercise of power at the expense of the poor.

Humphry Repton was the last of the great 18th-century landscape designers. His clients tended to be gentry or industrialists rather than aristocratic landowners, and his gardens therefore tended to be smaller in scale than those designed by Capability Brown. He was concerned, however, to assert the power and standing of his clients, and so often tried to create the illusion of a very large garden. This practice made entrance drives central to Repton's designs: his drives were long, sinuous, and indirect, often passing features of interest in his landscapes before a view of the house was afforded to the visitor.

The intentions underlying Repton's designs are better known than for any other designer of the period, because he produced for prospective clients 'Red Books' (so named because many were bound in red leather) that supplemented short written descriptions with his own watercolour paintings to contrast the gardens in their current state with his proposed gardens; his 'before and after' views were often facilitated by overlays consisting of folding flaps of paper. He produced more than 400 Red Books (not all of which led to commissions), of which at least 123 survive.

Repton's surviving gardens include Blaise Castle (near Bristol), for which he prepared a Red Book (now on display in Blaise Castle House) in 1796, in which he characteristically concentrated on the beauties of the winding drive, in which 'numberless beauties' would be 'brought before the eye in succession', together with 'the contrast of ascending and descending through a deep ravine of rich hanging woods'. In Jane Austen's *Northanger Abbey*, Isabella Thorpe memorably declared that Blaise Castle was 'the finest place in England'. In addition to commissions for estates, Repton also laid out several London squares, including Bloomsbury Square and the recently restored Russell Square.

The 19th century

Early 19th-century British gardens were mostly characterized by historical styles (including the landscape park), but one designer,

Sir Joseph Paxton, ventured imaginatively into the sphere of the glasshouse garden. In 1826, aged 23, he was appointed as head gardener at Chatsworth, where he altered Brown's design substantially, adding features such as an arboretum, a rock garden, and terraces with topiary. He also built glasshouses at Chatsworth, planting tropical fruit and tender ornamental plants; one of these houses was created to house the giant Amazon water lily (*Victoria amazonica*). In 1836 work began on the Great Conservatory (demolished 1920), which was the grandest glasshouse in England; its tropical garden was bisected by an indoor carriageway along which distinguished visitors were driven. This conservatory was the prototype of Paxton's greatest glasshouse, the Crystal Palace that he built in Hyde Park for the Great Exhibition of 1851. The interior was a display space rather than a garden, but it did incorporate mature trees that had been growing on the site. Paxton's many commissions included Birkenhead Park, on the Wirral peninsula, which was to prove a seminal influence on F. L. Olmsted, who went on to design many of America's greatest urban parks.

The late 19th and early 20th century was a period of innovation. The new feature that proved to be most enduring was the herbaceous border, a descendant of the French *plate-bande*. The first herbaceous borders are traditionally said to be the pair laid out at Arley Hall (Cheshire) in 1851, and they still survive. The high-maintenance demands of the herbaceous border meant that in the course of the 20th century it gradually gave way to the mixed border. There are exceptions, such as the fine herbaceous borders at Cliveden (Buckinghamshire) and Buckingham Palace, but the dominant form is now the mixed border, which contains both herbaceous and woody plants. The grandest example of the mixed border is the Long Border designed by Christopher Lloyd at Great Dixter (East Sussex), but there are countless examples of mixed borders in the suburban gardens of Britain.

The late 19th century also saw the rise of the woodland garden and the related form of the wild garden. The woodland garden was made possible by the availability of large flowering shrubs, particularly rhododendrons, magnolias, and camellias. The sites best suited to such plants were coastal areas with substantial rainfall, so woodland gardens were established in Cornwall (e.g. Trebah and Caerhays Castle) and the west of Scotland (e.g. Inverewe, in Wester Ross). In such gardens large shrubs were planted in woodland clearances and on coastal slopes, sometimes precipitous ones. The gardens are often designed to be viewed from a path running along the highest contour of a coastal garden.

The Victorian wild garden was in part a reaction against cultivars. The apostle of the movement was the Irish gardener and writer William Robinson, who championed the robustness of wild plants in wild settings in his bestselling *The Wild Garden* (1870) and its sequel, *The English Flower Garden* (1883). Woodland gardens had already begun to use bluebells as part of the settings for the large oriental shrubs, and Robinson extended the idea to other plants, especially bulbs (notably crocus and narcissus), which he planted in hay meadows. His own garden at Gravetye Manor in Surrey has been wonderfully preserved by the hotel that now owns the Manor.

In the 20th century the idea of the wild garden remained immensely influential. Robinson's advocacy of wild English roses, for example, was taken up by Gertrude Jekyll in her gardens and in her book on *Roses for English Gardens* (1902), and by Vita Sackville-West in her choice of wild roses for Sissinghurst. The notion of the wild garden lived on in the use of wild native plants in the gardens of Jens Jensen in America and Roberto Burle Marx in Brazil, and is now seen in the gardens of the New Perennial Movement, such as Piet Oudolf's 'Rivers of Grass' garden at the Trentham Estate in Staffordshire.

The 20th century

The dominant figure in garden design in late Victorian and Edwardian England was Gertrude Jekyll, who designed some 400 gardens. Just as Capability Brown had transformed the landscape garden, so Gertrude Jekyll created what was to become the quintessential English garden, with herbaceous borders, painterly planting, yew hedges, and climbing roses. About a third of her gardens were designed in collaboration with Edwin Lutyens, mostly between 1890 and 1910. This partnership created many of the greatest gardens in the Arts and Crafts tradition, which emphasized the use of vernacular materials and the structural arrangement of paths and plants.

One of the finest gardens that they designed together is Hestercombe, a Somerset estate with two historic gardens: an 18th-century garden and, on the other side of the house (but linked by the Daisy Steps designed by Lutyens), the garden laid out in 1904 by Jekyll and Lutyens and restored in the 1970s. At the centre of their garden is the Great Plat, a sunken parterre with triangular, stone-edged borders filled with bedding plants. The paths along two sides of the Great Plat are flanked by long rills planted with broadleaf arrowhead (*Sagittaria latifolia*). The paths lead to a pergola walk enveloped in wild roses, clematis, and honeysuckle.

One of the most influential Arts and Crafts gardens is Hidcote Manor (Gloucestershire), which the American plantsman Lawrence Johnston began to lay out in 1910. His planting is largely unknown, but the design features remain. Hidcote is an axial garden with a series of enclosures bordered with yew. These 'rooms' were widely imitated, perhaps most memorably at Sissinghurst (Kent), where Vita Sackville-West and Harold Nicolson created a garden around the fragmentary ruins of an Elizabethan manor house. They augmented existing enclosures with pleached limes and hedges of yew and box, and planted exuberantly; the enclosures often have gaps that afford glimpses of adjacent gardens. The influence of Gertrude Jekyll can be felt in the herbaceous borders, the drifts of colour, and the preference for wild roses.

The most famous of the individual gardens at Sissinghurst is the White Garden, which replaced an earlier rose garden in 1950. This garden, in which white flowers are set against luxuriant green foliage, inaugurated a fashion for the use of a thematic colour in planting design, and so became the principal vehicle for Jekyll's notion of how colour should be used in the garden. The National Trust assumed ownership of the garden in 1968, and the Trust's preference for clean lines and immaculate lawns has in some measure muted the cottage garden elements, but Sissinghurst rightly remains England's most celebrated 20th-century garden.

The cottage garden is a late Victorian romantic recreation of an imagined past in which healthy and contented cottage-dwellers cultivated densely planted artless gardens with an abundance of hollyhocks and roses. The form seems to have arisen from a tradition of watercolour paintings of idyllic cottage gardens, of which the best known exponent was Helen Allingham. The form was revived in the post-war years, largely because of the influence of Margery Fish's *We Made a Garden* (1956), which described the 'modest and unpretentious' cottage garden that she and her husband Walter had created at East Lambrook Manor (Somerset). This was very much a designed garden, with twisting paths and evergreen shrubs used to create structure, a lawn used to create a sense of openness, and a distinctive style of informal planting. The book and the garden both proved to be enormously influential, and the cottage garden became a way of asserting Englishness, both in heritage settings such as Anne Hathaway's Cottage, in a suburb of Stratford, and in distant British possessions: I have visited a cottage garden beside a farmhouse on an island in West Falkland, and another in Murree, a hill station near Islamabad.

In the 20th century the central feature of the domestic garden was the lawn. Lawn mowers had been manufactured since the 1830s, but they were too heavy for domestic use; many were drawn by horses. In the early 20th century the introduction of relatively light hand mowers brought the mower into the suburban garden, and the lawn became a carefully nurtured emblem of horticultural purity and precision, cut short (sometimes in a striped pattern), fed, weeded, scarified, aerated, and trimmed at the edges. Perhaps because machinery was involved, the lawn became part of the male domain and the well-kept lawn became a mark of responsible home ownership. In times of war, however, maintenance of a lawn was thought frivolous, and in both world wars Victory Gardens in which fruit and vegetables were grown were planted in public parks and on private lawns in Britain and around the world. These gardens freed resources for the military, and also raised morale by allowing non-combatants to contribute to the war effort.

Alongside vernacular gardens, Britain's designers have continued to create innovative gardens, often for public and corporate clients. In the post-war period, Brenda Colvin, Dame Sylvia Crowe, and Sir Geoffrey Jellicoe are among those who have designed important gardens and landscapes. Brenda Colvin, the founder of what is now the Landscape Institute, undertook hundreds of private commissions, notably Sutton Courtenay Manor House (Oxfordshire), but is primarily known for her large landscapes, which included the University of East Anglia, where she created settings for Denys Lasdun's buildings, Aldershot military town (Surrey), where she converted tarmac into woodland, and Gale Common (Yorkshire), where she converted a hill of coal ash generated by nearby power stations into a wooded landscape with earthworks that recall the ancient field systems still visible on England's chalk downs.

Sylvia Crowe shared an office with Brenda Colvin, but they seem never to have collaborated. Like Brenda Colvin, Dame Sylvia undertook private commissions, but her importance lies in her work on industrial landscapes and planned residential communities. At nuclear power stations in Wales (at Trawsfynydd, in Snowdonia, and Wylfa Head, in Anglesey), she revived the tradition of creating artificial hills, partly to conceal the lower-level buildings at the installations, but also to provide a suitable setting for the vast generators. The new towns for which she designed the landscaping included Harlow (Essex), Basildon (Essex), and Washington (Tyne and Wear). She also designed memorable recreational landscapes for reservoirs, notably Rutland Water.

Sir Geoffrey Jellicoe was creator of both modernist and historicist gardens. His first commission, in the wake of his book on *Italian Gardens of the Renaissance* (1925), was an axial Renaissance Revival garden at Ditchley (Oxfordshire). Thirty years later, in 1964, Jellicoe designed his most memorable British garden, the John F. Kennedy Memorial Garden at Runnymede (Surrey), on the site of the sealing of Magna Carta in 1215. In this garden Jellicoe imaginatively recreated Runnymede Field, in which he placed a flight of steps that lead gently upwards to the Kennedy memorial stone. The garden's influences include not only the notion of life's journey embodied in *The Pilgrim's Progress*, but also Carl Jung.

In this notion of the postmodernist garden, Jellicoe had an important successor in the poet and sculptor Ian Hamilton Finlay, whose Little Sparta (Lanarkshire) is the most important 20th-century garden in Scotland. This is on one level a garden of ideas—the French Revolution, World War II, the sea, Presocratic philosophy—but there is also a sense of challenge at work in the garden. In the inscriptions that proliferate in the garden, for example, there is none of the solemnity of the precedents in The Leasowes and Ermenonville, but rather a multiplicity of confrontations with the visitor in punning inscriptions such as 'Bring Back the Birch'. Engagements with literature in the garden include Lovers' Tree Plaques (e.g. Rosalind and Orlando, in Shakespeare's *As You Like It*) and Julie's Garden, a recreation of the Elysée garden in Rousseau's *Julie, ou la nouvelle Héloïse*.

Britain's contemporary designers work in a variety of styles. Kim Wilkie produces highly sculptural designs, notably his recreation of the pyramid mount in the garden of Boughton House, Northamptonshire. Within London, Wilkie's commissions include the vast redevelopment of Chelsea Barracks. He was also the designer of a sequence of five historically informed landscapes along the Thames (from Hampton to Kew). In Scotland, the most prominent exponent of sculptural design is the architect, designer, and sculptor Charles Jencks, whose best known creation is the large Garden of Cosmic Speculation at his home near Dumfries. The garden reflects Jencks's interest in contemporary cosmology. It is, like Little Sparta, a garden of ideas, but these ideas have led to a garden that resembles a sculpture park in which the sculptures are formed from the land.

In recent years the dominant style of designed British gardens has been minimalist, and the most prominent advocate of that style has been Christopher Bradley-Hole, whose gardens are distinctly geometrical, and often use the golden ratio (the classical *sectio aurea*) to determine proportion. He differs from some minimalists in his willingness to use plants, albeit for structural purposes rather than mere ornamentation. His most influential garden to date has been the minimalist Latin Garden that he designed in 1997 for the Chelsea Flower Show, which is often said to be the finest show garden ever to have been seen at Chelsea. It is also the garden that led Chelsea away from its tradition of Arts and Crafts gardens to a contemporary idiom. The garden was intended as a meditation on three stages in the life of the Roman poet Virgil: his rural childhood, his urban career, and his rural retirement. The design centred on a straight line marking the path of Virgil's life; the planting was simple, and in the case of the tall, thin conifers, successfully evoked the Roman campagna.

Britain's most visited garden is the Eden Project in Cornwall, which at its peak has attracted 1.5 million visitors a year. The site was a derelict industrial wasteland centred on a moribund china clay pit. The visionary client who could see the potential of this desolate land was Tim Smit, who commissioned the project. The site is now a designed landscape created by Dominic Cole, dominated by two elegant tripartite domes that are called biomes, designed by Sir Nicolas Grimshaw. The Rainforest Biome, which has a canopy walkway and a waterfall, is a habitat for plants such as coffee, cocoa, bananas, and rubber plants, and for tropical birds. The smaller Mediterranean Biome contains plants such as lemon trees, olive trees, and grape vines. The third planting area is the Outdoor Garden, which accommodates plants that can be grown outdoors in Cornwall and used for medicine, materials, food, and fuel. This 21st-century Garden of Eden aspires to recapture the spirit of the biblical Eden, where 'out of the ground made the Lord God to grow every tree that is pleasant to the sight and good for food'.

The Eden Project is a prominent product of the rise of ecologically informed planting and design, a movement championed in its early years by gardeners such as Beth Chatto, who emphasized the close association between site and the choice of plants, and is now best represented by the work of the academic and designer James Hitchmough, whose naturalistic designs and random plantings create plant communities that function ecologically.

In 21st-century Britain, gardening continues to be an important leisure activity: millions of people tend gardens and allotments, and millions visit gardens that are open to the public. Gardening has also become an armchair activity: gardening programmes proliferate on television, and there is nightly coverage of the show gardens at the Chelsea Flower Show. The public profile of the garden in contemporary Britain is indicative of its deep cultural imprint. The view (attributed to Napoleon) that Britain is a nation of shopkeepers reflects a jaundiced view of the country's commercial success, but one could make a good case for Britain being a nation of gardeners.

Chapter 9
America, Africa, and Australia

North America

Although the Indians of Central and South America had gardens, the indigenous peoples of North America farmed (mostly corn, squash, and beans), but did not have a comparable tradition of gardens. North America was colonized by four European countries—Spain, France, the Netherlands, and England—and settlers from these countries recreated the types of gardens with which they were familiar. The Spanish Franciscans who arrived in San Agustín (now St Augustine, Florida) in 1573 had a garden in their friary; this was probably the first garden in North America, but it does not survive. Such gardens, which were constructed in the cloisters of Franciscan and Dominican missions, would typically have included fruit trees, medicinal herbs, and a kitchen garden. The earliest surviving example of such a garden is the walled garden in the St Sulpice Seminary in Montréal, which was built in 1684; the extent to which the design of the garden reflects the original design is not clear.

In New Amsterdam (now New York), Pieter Stuyvesant, the last Director-General of New Netherland, laid out what may have been the first pleasure garden in America at his governor's house (built 1658) on the southern tip of Manhattan. This was a Dutch garden with an axis along which parterres, orchards, and a small canal were organized symmetrically. The equivalent residence of the Governor of New France was Château St Louis, in Quebec City. The first château on the site was built in 1648; it had a large kitchen garden, and also a place designated for relaxation. In 1694 a new château was built on the same site (now the site of the Château Frontenac Hotel), with formal French gardens extending to the south-west.

The English colonies, like their predecessors, drew on the traditions of the homeland. The most important surviving colonial garden in America is Middleton Place, a plantation near Charleston, South Carolina, commissioned in 1741 by Henry Middleton, the second president of the First Continental Congress. The design draws on the French formal garden of Le Nôtre. The axis descends from the site of the original house through six lawned terraces to two lakes (shaped like a butterfly, with the central *allée* as the thorax) and a canalized river.

Two other important colonial gardens survive, though not in their original form. One is the terraced garden of the Governor's Palace in Colonial Williamsburg. The garden is an imaginative recreation based loosely on early drawings and archaeological research, with an emphasis on American plants: the topiary, for example, is yaupon, an American holly. The Anglo-Dutch features of the garden (wholly appropriate to the reign of William and Mary) include a canal, a maze, and a mount.

The second garden is at Mount Vernon, George Washington's home on the Potomac River. Washington inherited the property in 1761. He soon rebuilt the house in a Palladian idiom (in wood), and later designed the garden, which occupies about a sixth of the estate. The garden has some of the characteristics of the English landscape garden; the lawn close to the house is, for example, separated from a deer park by a ha-ha. Washington's innovations included an approach road that was serpentine rather than straight, and so afforded glimpses of the house before it could be properly seen. The garden is very well documented, in part because Washington's own planting records have survived, and this plethora of detail has enabled the Mount Vernon Ladies' Association, which governs the property, to take the decision to restore the garden to its appearance in 1799, at the end of Washington's life. The result is a fine garden wholly appropriate to Washington's standing as a gentleman, a man of taste, and an American hero.

The greatest architectural legacy of the late colonial and early independence period is Monticello, the Virginia estate of Thomas Jefferson, whose capacious learning (based on reading in six languages) included a formidable knowledge of architecture, garden design, and botany. His knowledge of garden design was enhanced by his tour (with John Adams) of English gardens in 1786; they were particularly impressed by The Leasowes, in Halesowen. Jefferson began work on Monticello in 1768 by levelling a mountaintop, on which he built a house in the neoclassical style—the house featured on the American nickel.

The gardens consist of twenty oval flower beds, a 'Winding Flower Border' around the West Lawn, a lengthy (1,000 feet/300 metre) vegetable terrace, several orchards, and an ornamental forest called 'The Grove'. The design was innovative, but the garden was chiefly remarkable for its plants: Jefferson bought and traded plants all his life, secured new plants from the Lewis and Clark expedition to the Pacific, and constantly experimented with flowers, fruit, vegetables, and trees.

The new republic had egalitarian ideals, and so many of the great landscape projects of America's first century were designed to serve groups of citizens rather than individuals. Sometimes these were affluent citizens, as in the case of Llewellyn Park (New Jersey), America's first planned residential community (founded 1857), which is a collection of small estates with Romantic landscaping that included large trees, streams, ornamental shrubs, and lawns punctuated with America's first displays of naturalized crocus, narcissus, and jonquil. A decade later, F. L. Olmsted and his partner Calvert Vaux designed Riverside in a suburb of Chicago, where there is a mixture of grand and modest houses laid out on leafy curvilinear streets.

In such projects the landscape park had been reinvented as a model village. One lasting consequence of such integrated designs is that internal barriers were discouraged, so instead of walls and fences and hedges, there are lawns stretching to the street and few marked boundaries between individual properties. This is still a prominent feature of the American suburb, and distinguishes it sharply from the English suburb, where walls, fences, and hedges are much in evidence.

Frederick Law Olmsted was America's greatest landscape architect. His career began as the project manager responsible for implementing Calvert Vaux's design for New York's Central Park (1857–61). He subsequently formed a partnership with Vaux, and then worked with a succession of partners throughout the second half of the century. Of the approximately 500 projects that Olmsted completed, about two-thirds were in what would now be described as the public sector, and the others were gardens for the Gilded Age mansions of the tycoons who emerged in the closing decades of the 19th century.

Olmsted's parks and gardens were informed by his enthusiasm for 18th-century English gardens, the principles of which he understood through the prism of the writings of William Shenstone and William Gilpin. He was also guided by a conviction that the purpose of parks and gardens was respite, not aesthetic appreciation. In his parks he therefore eschewed elements that he thought merely decorative, such as flower beds, in favour of landscapes that could ease the tensions of urban life. When he had sufficient space at his disposal, his preferred idiom was what theorists of the time called the pastoral, which was a rolling landscape with clumps of trees and expanses of grass in which the visitor was encouraged to wander. The finest expression of Olmsted's pastoral landscapes is the Long Meadow that sweeps through the north and west sections of Prospect Park, in Brooklyn. With less space at his disposal, Olmsted used a picturesque style, most powerfully in the state park (America's first) on the American side of Niagara Falls, where Olmsted chose plants that would benefit from the spray.

Of Olmsted's commissions from the magnates of the Gilded Age, the best known is Biltmore, the North Carolina estate of George W. Vanderbilt, in the foothills of the Appalachians. The 250-room mansion is surrounded by a vast estate, of which Olmsted landscaped some 250 acres (100 hectares). The three mile (5 km) approach road winds over hills and through ravines, hedged in by a forest as thick as a jungle, and then the visitor is suddenly confronted with a full view of the vast mansion lying at the end of a huge manicured lawn. Beyond the mansion, the impression is altogether different, as the eye is drawn to descending terraces in the foreground and ascending mountains in the distance. The features of this part of the garden include a four acre (1.5 hectare) kitchen garden and a series of artfully designed (but convincingly naturalistic) wildflower meadows. The grand scale of the garden is a reflection of Vanderbilt's vast wealth, but is also a tribute to what Olmsted could achieve when unconstrained by considerations of space and budget. The Olmsted style became embedded in the American sense of what a park and a garden should be, and in the half century after Olmsted's retirement, his company attracted several thousand new commissions.

In the early 20th century, the wealthy family whose members had the greatest commitment to the creation of gardens was the Du Ponts, whose fortune was based on the chemical industry. In the 1920s, H. F. Du Pont began the process of transforming the family estate at Winterthur (Delaware) into a distinguished museum of American decorative arts. The garden that Du Pont created at Winterthur is America's greatest expression of the landscape garden. Its outstanding features include the imaginative use of woodland layers (ground cover, shrubs, small trees, and tall trees) to create perspectives onto the fields and meadows of the estate, and the cultivated illusion of wildness, in which native and exotic plants are arranged as if growing wild, but nonetheless present complementary and contrasting structures and colours.

Elsewhere in Delaware (near Wilmington) Alfred Du Pont developed a vast estate that he called Nemours, building a mansion in a late 18th-century French style and creating a formal French garden in the style of Versailles. The tree-lined Long Walk that forms its axis culminates in a one-acre pool surrounded by sculptures and fitted with a fountain that shoots water through 157 jets. In Pennsylvania (near Kennett Square), Pierre Du Pont created the Longwood Gardens, where twenty outdoor gardens (complemented by twenty gardens under glass) include a spectacular fountain garden (now being restored), a generous meadow garden, and (on the site of the kitchen garden) an educational facility that is now known as the Idea Garden.

Alongside the grand gardens of America's industrial magnates, the Colonial Revival movement was the inspiration for many gardens in a wholly different idiom. This movement, which has its origins in the Arts and Crafts movement, seems to have been inspired by the 1876 Centennial Exhibition in Philadelphia. In a sense the term 'Colonial Revival' is a misnomer, in that Colonial Revival gardens are not historical reconstructions as much as evocative romantic recreations. The revival element consists of rectangular beds and straight paths, but the planting is not historical: colonial beds were used for fruit and vegetables, but Colonial Revival beds are planted with flowers. Similarly, the iconic picket fence once used in colonial gardens to protect the borders from hungry animals has been replaced with box, but picket fences (usually painted white) are often deployed as a historical gesture elsewhere in the gardens.

The best known examples of Colonial Revival gardens are clustered around Washington, DC: Arlington House (General Lee's house, now in Arlington National Cemetery), Mount Vernon (George Washington's House), and the Old Stone House in the Georgetown area (in which the entire garden is encompassed by a picket fence). The outstanding national example of the Colonial Revival garden is Colonial Williamsburg, where the landscape architect (Arthur Shurcliff) used archaeological research to recover hard surfaces and postholes, but used his educated imagination in his choice of plants.

The principal successor to the gardens of the Colonial Revival was the Prairie School, which championed the use of indigenous plants. The best known members of the Prairie School were the landscape architect Jens Jensen and the architect Frank Lloyd Wright. Jensen's most important private gardens were commissioned by members of the Ford family. His commissions for Henry and Clara Ford included many of their charitable projects, and their family estate, Fair Lane (in Dearborn, Michigan). The features of Fair Lane include an axial meadow with a gap in the trees aligned to capture sunset at the summer solstice. For Edsel (Henry's son) and Eleanor Ford, Jensen designed Gaukler Point (on Lake St Clair, in Michigan), Haven Hill (in southern Michigan), and Skylands (in Seal Harbor, Maine, now Martha Stewart's summer house).

The signature features of Jensen's gardens include designed floral compositions consisting mainly of indigenous plants, and a lengthy entrance road in which the views of the house are delayed and then intermittent. Frank Lloyd Wright's gardens can be relatively formal, as at Taliesin West (Arizona), where the indoor and outdoor spaces are ingeniously integrated, which means that the gardens reflect the structures of the buildings. At the other extreme, at Fallingwater (Pennsylvania), perhaps the greatest triumph of domestic architecture in 20th-century America, the planting is so naturalistic that the garden seems to fade imperceptibly into the surrounding forest (see Figure 15).

15. Fallingwater, Pennsylvania.

In the mid-20th century the California Style of garden design emerged, driven by the functionalist values of modernism: simplicity, abstract forms, hard surfaces, and a principled resistance to the idea of a garden having a beginning or an end, or having the axial and architectural features still being championed in the historicized Beaux-Arts gardens then in fashion. The apostle of the California Style was Thomas Church, whose travels in Europe had stimulated his interests in cubism. His greatest garden, built in the late 1940s, is the Donnell Garden at El Novillero (Sonoma), which is rightly acclaimed as one of the greatest gardens of the century. The approach road follows the austere rocky route of a former cattle trail ('novillero' means 'cattle pen'). The ideology of cubism can be seen most clearly in the multiplicity of viewing points, and in the curvilinear freeform swimming pool, which is set at an unexpected angle with respect to the surrounding redwood decking, which is constructed around the trunks of mature trees.

The California Style was well suited to small gardens, and its embracing of hard surfaces led to the easy accommodation of cars in the front garden and patios, decks, and swimming pools in the back yard. In the post-war years the style spread to suburbs all across America, even to states in which outdoor living was only possible for part of the year. Within urban centres, gardens took a different trajectory, and innovative gardens sprang up on rooftops, in shopping plazas, and small ('vest pocket') parks.

The wartime Victory Gardens that transformed ornamental public and private gardens into vegetable patches evolved into community gardens, of which there are now thousands of examples. Some community gardens are planned, officially sanctioned spaces, but most are joyously illicit appropriations of derelict land transformed by neighbourhood groups into urban oases with trees and seating and vegetable plots and birdsong. The pioneer of the guerrilla garden movement was Liz Christy, whose band of Green Guerrillas planted a community garden in the Bowery area of Manhattan in 1973. The Liz Christy Community Garden, as it is now known, proved to be the fuse that lit a national movement, and her Green Guerrillas became the prototype of informal associations of seed-bombing gardeners all over the United States and in dozens of countries around the world.

In the sphere of grand gardens, the late 20th century witnessed the gradual displacement of the private client by civic and corporate clients. The many landscape architects in this sphere included Dan Kiley and Lawrence Halprin. Kiley's designs combined historicist elements (often drawn from 17th-century French gardens) with modernist features. His civic gardens include the Henry Moore Sculpture Garden for the Nelson-Atkins Museum of Art in Kansas City, and his corporate commissions include the indoor garden at the Ford Foundation in New York City. Lawrence Halprin, who trained with Thomas Church at the Donnell Garden, was an innovative designer whose finest creation is the memorial to Franklin Delano Roosevelt in Washington, DC. The memorial is a sequence of four garden rooms organized in a narrative sequence to illustrate the history of the USA during Roosevelt's four terms of office.

In the 21st century, American designers continue to produce wonderful gardens. In the creation of parks, Olmsted's most distinguished successor is arguably Michael Van Valkenburgh. In the gardens of the New Perennial Movement, the leading figures are Adam Woodruff and Benjamin Futa. The most remarkable radical innovator in contemporary American landscape design is Martha Schwartz, who brings to her urban landscape installations the ironic tone of contemporary art, especially pop art. Her landscapes, which sometimes use neither plants nor water, regenerate urban space. One particularly fine example is the plaza in front of Marcel Breuer's brutalist building that accommodates the Department of Housing and Urban Development in Washington, DC: seven canopies that resemble flying saucers hover above discs that support mounds of grass. The boldness of the design was compromised by the conservative tastes of the client, so the canopies, which were to be brightly coloured, are blandly white, but the effect of the installation is nonetheless a tribute to the vibrancy of the design.

Central and South America

The most important gardens in Central America are in Mexico, where the gardens include the Bosque de Chapultepec (Woodland of Grasshopper Hill), a remnant of Motecuhzuma I's royal garden. The site remained accessible to the public after the Conquest, and in the 19th century the sides of the hill (which is surmounted by an 18th-century castle) were terraced, and the grounds laid out as a landscape park. In the early 20th century the garden was again remodelled, this time in the style of the Bois de Boulogne in Paris, and in the 1960s and 1970s the size of the park was doubled. It now functions as Mexico City's lung, attracting some fifteen million visitors a year to its cultural attractions (museums and a zoo), recreational facilities, and green spaces. The trees include many Montezuma cypress (Mexican swamp cypress), some of which were planted by the Aztecs.

In the 1940s, Mexico began to shrug off its colonial inheritance in garden design and to create a distinctive national style. The inspirational leader of this process was the architect Luis Barragán, who in the 1940s changed the focus of his work from housing to landscape architecture. His most celebrated landscape is the Parque Residencia Jardines del Pedregal de San Ángel. El Pedregal, as it is popularly known, was built on a lava field, and its luxuriant gardens take full advantage of the sculptural quality of the lava formations in which they are set. The minimalist abstract buildings of El Pedregal have large windows from which the occupants can see artfully constructed gardens that appear to be wild.

Until the mid-20th century, the gardens of South America tended to be built in European styles, albeit with some indigenous planting. The Parque Forestal in Santiago (Chile), for example, resembles an English landscape garden, and it once had a lake with a balustraded promenade. Similarly, Palacio Bosch, a French neoclassical mansion in Buenos Aires (now the residence of the American ambassador), has a magnificent French neoclassical garden with fine *parterres de broderie*. Estancia Acelain, the most distinguished *estancia* (ranch) garden in Argentina, has a Mozarabic house with extensive Hispano-Islamic gardens modelled on those of the Alhambra.

The move away from European styles was led by the Brazilian plantsman and designer (and painter, sculptor, musician, and set designer) Roberto Burle Marx, who created a contemporary modernist style that has had a global influence. Burle Marx brought to design a prodigious knowledge of the flora of Brazil. He catalogued tens of thousands of plants and used his estate, now known as the Sítio Roberto Burle Marx, as a research laboratory in which he grew some 3,500 species of Brazilian flora. The gardens that Burle Marx designed are characterized by a broad range of native plants, often arranged by colour or species, and by an eclectic use of Amerindian, African, and colonial styles. In his gardens he tried to create rhythms of colour and texture, and to relate their structures to their settings. Burle Marx undertook some 2,000 commissions, of which his best known are probably the Paseo de Copacabana and the Parque do Flamengo, both in Rio de Janeiro, and Gilberto Strunk Residence, in Petrópolis.

The Paseo de Copacabana, which is the promenade of Copacabana Beach, is a long pavement landscape articulated in a design that resembles a geometrical wave. The Parque do Flamengo was another shoreline project, a landfill site in the area between central Rio and Copacabana. Burle Marx's responsibility within this large collaborative project was the design of the gardens and civic landscapes. Burle Marx divided the site into eleven zones, and chose the shrubs, trees, and palms for each section, often placing the plants in homogeneous botanical groups. The 16,000 specimens that he planted were drawn from some 250 species, and herbaceous plants were for the most part excluded. Hard surfaces include a winding stone mosaic that passes through the garden like a river. The Gilberto Strunk Residence has a house (designed by Oscar Niemeyer) with a roofline suggestive of a rope bridge spanning the valley. In Burle Marx's adjoining garden, a crimson river of Bloodleaf (*Iresine*) appears to flow under the bridge. The use of contrasting colours creates a landscape that seems to be painted with plants. It is by any measure one of the world's finest private gardens, a tribute to the creativity and inventive powers of one of the greatest designers of the 20th century.

Sub-Saharan Africa

In sub-Saharan Africa, the country with the longest tradition of gardening is South Africa. The oldest surviving garden is the Company's Garden, which is beside the Parliament Building in Cape Town. The 'Company' is the Dutch East India Company, which founded the garden in 1652 to grow fruit and vegetables for the victualling of ships. The only survivor of this original garden is an ancient pear tree. When the Company was declared bankrupt in 1798, the garden became derelict. It was gradually restored, and in 1848 was reopened as a botanic garden specializing in local flora. The beds of flowers from southern Africa have now been supplemented with a rose garden, a Japanese garden, a herb garden, and a rockery.

As in America, the magnates of South Africa, whose wealth was based on mining, commissioned gardens. The finest surviving magnate garden is Brenthurst, in Parktown (Johannesburg), which was built for Sir Drummond Chaplin in 1904. The garden that he commissioned had terraces, a rock garden, and an abundance of water; the avenue of planes planted when the house was being built still survives. In 1922 the estate passed to the

Oppenheimer family, and Henry and Bridget Oppenheimer employed Joane Pim, South Africa's greatest garden designer, to refashion the gardens. Pim's design retained water as a central feature, but replaced European plants with indigenous ones, and populated the garden with sculptures. The garden is still maintained by the Oppenheimers, and is run on what the family describes as holistic principles: there is no watering, the lawns (of African grasses) are ankle-high, and no pesticides are used.

Elsewhere in South Africa, the most notable gardens are in Stellenbosch. The Old Nectar Gardens near Stellenbosch are the creation of Una van der Spuy, who tended them for seventy-one years, until her death at the age of one hundred in 2012. The gardens are bordered by venerable oak trees, and consist of a series of small garden rooms (like Hidcote, in England), including a rose garden and a waterfall garden; the most recent additions are a terraced garden and an indigenous garden.

At Rustenberg, an estate rightly associated with its excellent wine, there is a 21st-century garden, commissioned by Rozanne Barlow. The garden is contemporary, but draws on an eclectic range of traditions. The structural element consists of paths that divide the garden into four sections. In one section a tennis court has been replaced by a labyrinth (modelled on the one in Chartres Cathedral) of brick and river stone. And in a gesture towards the 'borrowed landscape' of the gardens of China and Japan, there are unimpeded views of the estate's vineyards and of the mountains in the distance. All of this can be enjoyed with a glass of Rustenberg wine.

Australia

The oldest garden in Australia, on the site of what is now the Royal Botanic Gardens in Sydney, was (like the Company's Garden in Cape Town) intended for the provisioning of ships. The development of the site began with the establishment of a grain farm in 1788, and soon mixed farms extended the area that was to become the botanic garden. The aspiration to use the site for recreation, first articulated by the governor in 1810, was realized when the botanic garden was founded in 1816. In the two succeeding centuries, the garden has evolved continually, slowly moving away from the early emphasis on English plants in favour of Australia's native flora. There are now many themed gardens, including a Herb Garden, a Palm Grove, a Rare and Threatened Plants Garden, a Fernery, and an Australian Native Rockery.

In the late 19th and early 20th century, Australia's most important botanist and garden designer was William Guilfoyle, who was apprenticed in the nursery run by his father (who had been trained by Sir Joseph Paxton). In the public sector, Guilfoyle's principal achievement was the remodelling of what are now the Royal Botanic Gardens in Melbourne. In 1873 Guilfoyle was appointed to the directorship of the Gardens in succession to the botanist Baron Sir Ferdinand von Mueller, who had laid out the garden in accordance with botanical principles of kinship. Guilfoyle created a wholly new design, moving thousands of his predecessor's trees and creating flower beds, lawns, promenades, and a large lake. He planted many date palms, and favoured plants such as yuccas for their structural qualities. The vistas that he created were conceived in the tradition of the picturesque garden, and they remain one of the glories of the Gardens today. Guilfoyle also undertook many private commissions, of which the best known is Mawallok (Victoria), which he designed in 1909; it was his last commission, and perhaps his greatest garden. The plains of western Victoria are windy, so the house and garden are protected by large conifers marshalled into windbreaks, and there are strategically placed hedges and stone walls.

In the 20th century, Australia's most important and influential garden designer was Edna Walling, who in the 1920s developed a powerful and distinctive style that was to characterize her hundreds of commissions for half a century. Her gardens were strongly architectural, both in the scale and layout of structures that she incorporated into them (colonnades, balustrades, stairs, pergolas, pools, and walls, often covered with climbing plants) and in her carefully meditated plantings (which often included a deliberately unstructured 'wild' area with Australian plants). She favoured a narrow palette of colours, with an emphasis on green with an admixture of pastels. The overall effect for which she strove was a succession of picturesque spaces.

One of Walling's best preserved gardens is Markdale (Binda, New South Wales), whose features include winding paths with a planned succession of views, and a pergola (a survivor from an earlier garden) that she planted with wisteria and roses and supplemented with a sunken rose garden at one end. The impact of Walling's gardens on the contemporary Australian garden can still be felt, in part because it was widely disseminated through her books and her regular articles in Australian *Home Beautiful*.

Postscript: the future history of the garden

Planting and garden design have never stood still, in part because fashions change, but also because of external factors. The most conspicuous fashion in recent decades has been the rise of organic gardening, a movement originating in the 1920s and energized by the publication in 1962 of Rachel Carson's *Silent Spring*, which excoriated the use of chemical pesticides, weedkillers, and fertilizers. In recent decades, the antipathy towards 'chemicals' (the term is used disparagingly, as if we were not all made of chemicals) has been extended to genetically modified plants, which are presented as Frankenstein flora. In its present state, organic gardening aspires to sustainability achieved by a synergy with natural systems of soil enrichment and pest and disease control. It is entirely unclear whether the trajectory of growth will continue (in agriculture as well as gardens), or whether the fashion will wither. The element of organic gardening that seems most likely to survive in the long term is sustainability, as that is rooted in solid science rather than a counter-cultural mistrust of science.

Another driver of change is the reduction in biodiversity. The rapid rate of species extinction that threatens biodiversity is driven by a series of factors known by the acronym HIPPO: habitat loss, invasive species, pollution, population growth, and overexploitation. Gardens are part of the solution, in that gardeners often provide a sustaining environment for species that are threatened, but gardens are also part of the problem: nurseries import plants from all over the world, and a plant that is well integrated in its homeland can wreak horticultural havoc in a new environment, and so become an invasive species. In Britain, Japanese knotweed was declared in 1847 to be the most interesting new ornamental plant of the year, and then sold through nurseries; now it destroys gardens.

HIPPO factors are entirely human in origin. In the case of climate change, a natural phenomenon is accelerated by human action. Winters in temperate climates will be wetter and sometimes colder, which will not suit many plants. Such conditions are, however, ideal for fungal diseases. The other three seasons will be warmer and drier, and that too will not be ideal for many plants. The ever-increasing shortages of water, which in some parts of the world are exacerbated by the practice of drawing river water upstream and so depleting water supplies downstream, will inevitably have an effect on gardens as well as agriculture.

These changes will certainly affect gardens. In England, for example, traditional garden plants such as roses and lupins are likely to be replaced by Mediterranean plants, which will be accompanied by Mediterranean pests. Casualties will include the cottage garden, the yew hedge, and, in particular, the lawn. The lawn has long benefited from England's maritime climate and the solicitous ministrations of amateur gardeners, and many a modest house has a healthy and tidy lawn that is a source of pride. The beauty of the English lawn is dependent on moderate temperatures and an abundant supply of water, and both are slowly disappearing. Rising summer temperature and less summer rainfall creates a need to use more water at a time when water is being informally rationed by ever-increasing prices and on occasion formally rationed by hosepipe bans. The increasing use of grey water (sometimes called 'sullage') will retard the gradual diminishing of the water supply, but gardeners will have to shower many times a day to produce enough grey water to keep a lawn green. In dry places such as California, lawns are particularly thirsty, and require regular ministrations of chemicals to maintain their appearance. It seems likely that in the course of the 21st century, lawns will become an extravagance associated with conspicuous expenditure, and possibly a marker of anti-societal greed.

Landscape architects and garden designers are increasingly responsive to climate change. The new horticultural science of xeriscaping (gardening with a reduced need for water) often involves replacing lawns with plants that require little water. For the same reasons, hard landscaping is an increasingly dominant feature in design. Ecologically informed garden design was once a fringe enthusiasm, but has now moved to the mainstream. In short, gardens will continue to evolve, as they have since remote antiquity. And just as adaptation to ensure survival is an integral part of any business strategy, so garden design will adapt to changing conditions, and gardens will continue to provide havens of beauty and respite for the weary. Perhaps in the gardens of the future there will be occasional shady bowers for garden historians, many of whom would endorse Cicero's view that *si hortum in bibliotheca habes, deerit nihil*: if you have a garden in your library, you will have everything you need.

Glossary

allée A straight path or tree-lined avenue in a formal garden.

arboretum A place set aside for the exhibition of a collection of trees.

arbour (or arbor) A bower or shady retreat, of which the sides and roof are formed by trees and shrubs closely planted or intertwined, or of lattice work covered with climbing shrubs and plants.

automaton (plural automata) In gardens, devices such as singing birds, water organs, and mechanisms ('fire engines') that sprayed water at those who accidentally triggered them.

avenue In early use, the principal approach to a country house, usually bordered by trees; in later use, an alignment of trees.

azulejo (Spanish and Portuguese) A glazed polychrome tile.

belvedere In Italian, a viewing point. In English, with reference to gardens, an ornamental summer-house erected on a site that commands a good view.

bosco (plural *boschi*) and (French) *bosquet* An ornamental grove, usually with a lawn and fountain at the centre. The enclosed space within a bosquet was a *salle de verdure* (a green room) if it was large and a *cabinet de verdure* if it was small. The *bosquet à l'anglais* was a lawned area. In English a bosquet (sometimes spelt 'bosket') denoted an area of a garden planted with shrubs or small trees.

botanical garden A garden devoted to the study of plants.

canal A rectangular pool, usually long and narrow, often marking the central axis of the garden.

carpet-bedding (or mosaïculture) A bed in which dwarf foliage plants of similar size but different colour are arranged to form a pattern resembling a carpet.

chahar bagh Persian term meaning 'four rivers' (on the Indian subcontinent usually written as 'charbagh'), used to denote the cross-axial gardens of ancient Persia, in which the axes were delineated by intersecting irrigation channels.

chinoiserie A type of European art (including garden art) dominated by Chinese or pseudo-Chinese ornamental motifs.

eye-catcher An ornamental garden building or large statue designed to direct the gaze, typically at the end of an *allée* or at the top of a hill.

fabrique In French gardens, an ornamental structure.

ferme ornée ('ornamented farm') A working farm (not an ornamental farm) to which ornamental features have been added.

folly A garden building (such as a pagoda or a column or a hermitage) that is primarily ornamental rather than functional.

gallery A covered space for walking in a garden.

gazebo A garden building commanding an extensive view, possibly a jocular Latinism ('I shall gaze') analogous to *lavabo* ('I shall wash').

giardino segreto (Italian 'secret garden') A small enclosed garden, sometimes with a pavilion.

giochi d'aqua (Italian 'water games') Devices designed to drench unsuspecting visitors, known in French as as *jeux d'eau* and in Spanish as *burladores*.

grotto An artificial rusticated cave, typically containing fountains and decorated with statues and shells.

grove A group of trees forming shaded avenues or walks. The *bosco* and the wilderness are types of grove.

ha-ha A garden boundary designed to be invisible from the house, normally a walled ditch.

hortus conclusus (Latin 'enclosed garden') An enclosed garden, in the Middle Ages deemed to represent the virginity of Mary.

knot garden (French *entrelacs*) A small garden laid out in a series of continuous interlacing low hedges, typically planted with box.

Mannerism A late Renaissance style characterized by elongated shapes and a taste for novelty.

mirador Spanish term denoting a balcony, and (in later use) a garden building that commands a view. The term is equivalent to a belvedere or a gazebo.

mount An artificial hill in a garden.

obelisk A tall, tapering, four-sided, usually monolithic pillar or column of stone, revived from ancient Egypt.

orangery (French *orangerie*) A large conservatory in which oranges and other citrus fruits could be grown in northern climates.

pagoda An ornamental garden building in the form of a multi-tiered tower with storeys of diminishing size, each with an ornamented projecting roof.

parterre (French *par terre* 'on the ground') A flat ornamental flower garden laid out in geometrical or botanical designs. *Parterres de broderie* (Italian *ricami*) are 'embroidered' with symmetrical designs of box. *Parterres de pièces coupées* (cutwork parterres) consist of flowerbeds rather than box. *Parterres d'eau* used water as a prominent design component. *Parterres à l'anglaise*, which were called 'plats' in England, were constructed with cut turf (*gazon coupé*) set against coloured stones or soil.

pavilion An ornamental garden building, designed for temporary shelter or refreshment, and situated to afford views of the garden.

physic garden A garden for the cultivation of medicinal plants.

plate-bande In 17th-century French gardens, a strip-shaped flowerbed; in later use, a strip of grass.

pleasure garden Used in a general sense to denote a garden designed for pleasure rather than utility and in a particular sense to denote an ornamental urban garden open to the public.

potager French term for a kitchen garden, used in English to denote an ornamental kitchen garden; in French such a garden is described as a *potager décoratif*.

rill A channel of flowing water.

rococo Eighteenth-century decorative style marked by asymmetry and the use of shell-like and watery forms.

theatre (Italian *teatro de vedura*, French *théâtre de verdure*) An ornamental or functional garden theatre, with an architectural background of clipped hedges.

topiary The clipping and training of evergreen plants into ornamental or fantastic shapes.

Further reading

General

Cooper, David, *A Philosophy of Gardens* (Oxford, 2006).
Garden History (journal of the Garden History Society, from 1972).
Gothein, Marie Luise, *A History of Garden Art* (2 vols, English translation, London, 1928).
Hunt, John Dixon (ed.), 'Gardens', in *The Dictionary of Art* (Oxford and New York, 2003); available electronically as *Grove Art Online*.
Hunt, John Dixon, *Greater Perfections: The Practice of Garden History* (London, 2000).
Jellicoe, Geoffrey Alan, and Jellicoe, Susan, *The Landscape of Man* (London, 1995).
Leslie, Michael, and John Dixon Hunt (eds), *A Cultural History of Gardens* (6 vols, London, 2013).
Moore, Charles W., Mitchell, William J., and Turnbull, William, *The Poetics of Gardens* (Cambridge, MA, 1993).
Mosser, Monique, and Teyssot, Georges (eds), *The History of Garden Design: The Western Tradition from the Renaissance to the Present Day* (London, 1990).
Schama, Simon, *Landscape and Memory* (New York, 1995).
Studies in the History of Gardens and Designed Landscapes (formerly *Journal of Garden History*, from 1980).
Taylor, Patrick, *The Oxford Companion to the Garden* (Oxford, 2006).
Turner, Tom, *Garden History: Philosophy and Design 2000 BC–2000 AD* (London, 2005).

Chapter 1: The ancient and medieval garden

The Near East and eastern Mediterranean

Carroll, Maureen, *Earthly Paradises: Ancient Gardens in History and Archaeology* (London, 2003).

Dalley, Stephanie, *The Mystery of the Hanging Garden of Babylon* (Oxford, 2013).

Jashemski, Wilhelmina F., *The Gardens of Pompeii, Herculaneum and the Villas Destroyed by Vesuvius* (2 vols, New Rochelle, NY, 1979).

MacDougall, Elizabeth (ed.), *Ancient Roman Gardens* (Washington, DC, 1981).

MacDougall, Elizabeth (ed.), *Ancient Roman Villa Gardens* (Washington, DC, 1987).

Stackelberg, Katharine von, *The Roman Garden: Space, Sense and Society* (London, 2009).

Wilber, Donald Newton, *Persian Gardens and Garden Pavilions* (2nd edn, Washington, DC, 1979).

Wilkinson, Alix, *The Garden in Ancient Egypt* (London, 1998).

South Asia

Bopearachchi, Osmund, *The Pleasure Gardens of Sigiriya* (Colombo, 2006).

The medieval garden

Crisp, Frank, *Mediaeval Gardens* (2 vols, London, 1924).

Harvey, John, *Mediaeval Gardens* (London, 1981).

MacDougall, Elizabeth (ed.), *Medieval Gardens* (Washington, DC, 1986).

Byzantium

Bodin, Helena, and Hedlund, Ragnar (eds), *Byzantine Gardens and Beyond* (Uppsala, 2013).

Littlewood, Antony, Maguire, Henry, and Wolschke-Bulmahn, Joachim (eds), *Byzantine Garden Culture* (Washington, DC, 2002).

Central and South America

Aghajanian, Alfred, *Chinampas* (2nd edn, Los Angeles, 2007).

Chapter 2: The Islamic garden

Brookes, John, *Gardens of Paradise: The History and Design of the Great Islamic Gardens* (London, 1987).

MacDougall, Elizabeth, and Ettinghausen, Richard (eds), *The Islamic Garden* (Washington, DC, 1976).

Petruccioli, Attilio (ed.), *Gardens in the Time of the Great Muslim Empires: Theory and Design* (Leiden, 1997).

Ruggles, D. Fairchild, *Islamic Gardens and Landscapes* (Philadelphia, 2008).

The Mughal garden

Crowe, Sylvia, and Haywood, Sheila, *The Gardens of Mughul India* (London, 1972).

Moynihan, Elizabeth B. (ed.), *The Moonlight Garden: New Discoveries at the Taj Mahal* (Washington, DC, 2001).

Tillotson, Giles, *Taj Mahal* (Cambridge, MA, 2008).

Wescoat, James L., Jr, and Wolschke-Bulmahn, Joachim (eds), *Mughal Gardens: Sources, Places, Representations and Prospects* (Washington, DC, 1996).

Central Asia

Golombek, Lisa, 'The Gardens of Timur: New Perspectives', *Muqarnas*, 12 (1995), 137–47.

Iran

Hobhouse, Penelope, *Gardens of Persia* (London, 2003).

Khansari, Mehdi, Moghtader, M. Reza, and Yavari, Minouch (eds), *The Persian Garden: Echoes of Paradise* (Washington, DC, 1998).

Porter, Yves, and Thévenart, Arthur, *Palaces and Gardens of Persia* (English translation, London, 2003).

Wilbur, Donald, *Persian Gardens and Garden Pavilions* (2nd edn, Washington, DC, 1979).

The Middle East

Conan, Michel (ed.), *Middle East Garden Traditions: Unity and Diversity* (Washington, DC, 2007).

Hamilton, R. W., *Khirbat al-Mafjar: An Arabian Mansion in the Jordan Valley* (Oxford, 1959).

The Ottoman Empire

Atasoy, Nurhan, *A Garden for the Sultan: Gardens and Flowers in the Ottoman Culture* (English translation, Istanbul, 2002).

Spain and Portugal

Ruggles, D. Fairchild, *Gardens, Landscape and Vision in the Palaces of Islamic Spain* (University Park, PA, 2000).

Chapter 3: The East Asian garden

China

Clunas, Craig, *Fruitful Sites: Garden Culture in Ming Dynasty China* (London, 1996).

Congzhou, Chen, *On Chinese Gardens* (Shanghai, 1984).

Hay, John, *Kernels of Energy, Bones of Earth: The Rock in Chinese Art* (New York, 1985).

Henderson, Ron, *The Gardens of Suzhou* (Philadelphia, 2013).

Hu, Jie, *The Splendid Chinese Garden: Origins, Aesthetic and Architecture* (New York, 2013).

Keswick, Maggie, *The Chinese Garden: History, Art and Architecture* (3rd edn, London and Cambridge, MA, 2003).

Liyao, Cheng, *Ancient Chinese Architecture: Imperial Gardens* (English translation, Vienna, 1998).

Liyao, Cheng, *Ancient Chinese Architecture: Private Gardens* (English translation, Vienna, 1999).

Japan

Itoh, Teiji, *The Gardens of Japan* (2nd edn, London and Tokyo, 1998).

Kawaguchi, Yoko, *Japanese Zen Gardens* (London, 2014).

Kuck, Loraine, *The World of the Japanese Garden: From Chinese Origins to Modern Landscape Art* (New York, 1968).

Nitschke, Günter, *The Architecture of the Japanese Garden: Right Angle and Natural Form* (English translation, Cologne, 1991).

Chapter 4: Italy

Attlee, Helena, *Italian Gardens: A Cultural History* (London, 2006).

Beneš, Mirka, and Harris, Dianne, *Villas and Gardens in Early Modern Italy and France* (Cambridge, 2001).

Coffin, David, *The Villa d'Este at Tivoli* (Princeton, 1960).

Coffin, David (ed.), *The Italian Garden* (Washington, DC, 1972).

Coffin, David, *Gardens and Gardening in Papal Rome* (Princeton, 1991).

Dernie, David, *The Villa d'Este at Tivoli* (London, 1996).

Fabiani Giannetto, Raffaella, *Medici Gardens: From Making to Design* (Philadelphia, 2008).

Hobhouse, Penelope, with Giorgio Galletti, *Gardens of Italy* (London, 1998).

Hunt, John Dixon (ed.), *The Italian Garden: Art, Design and Culture* (Cambridge, 1996).

Lazzaro, Claudia, *The Italian Renaissance Garden* (New Haven, 1990).

Masson, Georgina, *Italian Gardens* (London, 1961).

Chapter 5: France

Adams, William Howard, *The French Garden, 1500–1800* (New York, 1979).

Beneš, Mirka, and Harris, Dianne, *Villas and Gardens in Early Modern Italy and France* (Cambridge, 2001).

Hazlehurst, F. Hamilton, *Gardens of Illusion: The Genius of André Le Nostre* (Nashville, TN, 1980).

Hunt, John Dixon, and Conan, Michel (eds), *Tradition and Innovation in French Garden Art* (Philadelphia, 2002).

Imbert, Dorothée, *The Modernist Garden in France* (New Haven, 1993).

Le Dantec, Denise, and Jean-Pierre, *Reading the French Garden: Story and History* (2nd edn, Cambridge, MA, 1993).

Thompson, Ian H., *The Sun King's Garden* (London, 2006).

Wiebenson, Dora, *The Picturesque Garden in France* (Princeton, 1978).

Woodbridge, Kenneth, *Princely Gardens: The Origins and Development of the French Formal Style* (London, 1986).

Chapter 6: Spain and Portugal

Attlee, Helena, *The Gardens of Portugal* (London, 2008).

Bowe, Patrick, *Gardens of Portugal* (New York, 1989).

Casa Valdés, Teresa Ozores, and Saavedra, Marquesa de, *Spanish Gardens* (English translation, London, 1987).

Segall, Barbara, *Gardens of Spain and Portugal* (London, 1999).

Chapter 7: Northern Europe

The Low Countries

Hunt, John Dixon (ed.), *The Dutch Garden in the Seventeenth Century* (Washington, DC, 1990).

Jacques, David, and van der Horst, Arend Jan, *The Gardens of William and Mary* (London, 1988).

Jong, Erik de, *Nature and Art: Dutch Garden and Landscape Architecture, 1650–1740* (Philadelphia, 2000).

Sellers, Vanessa Bezemer, *Courtly Gardens in Holland, 1600–1650: The House of Orange and the Hortus Batavus* (Amsterdam and Woodbridge, 2001).

Germany
Rohde, Michael (ed.), *Prussian Gardens in Europe: 300 Years of Garden History* (Leipzig, 2007).

Russia
Floryan, Margrethe, *Gardens of the Tsars* (Aarhus, 1996).
Hayden, Peter, *Russian Parks and Gardens* (London, 2005).

Chapter 8: Britain

Bisgrove, Richard, *The Gardens of Gertrude Jekyll* (London, 1992).
Brown, Jane, *Vita's Other World: A Garden Biography of V. Sackville-West* (Harmondsworth and New York, 1985).
Chambers, Douglas, *The Planters of the English Landscape Garden* (New Haven and London, 1993).
Daniels, Stephen, *Humphry Repton: Landscape Gardening and the Geography of Georgian England* (New Haven and London, 1999).
Elliott, Brent, *Victorian Gardens* (Portland and London, 1986).
Hadfield, Miles, *A History of British Gardening* (London, 1985).
Hunt, John Dixon, *Garden and Grove: The Italian Renaissance Garden in the English Imagination, 1600–1750* (London, 1986).
Hunt, John Dixon, *William Kent: Landscape Garden Designer* (London, 1987).
Hunt, John Dixon, *The Figure in the Landscape: Poetry, Painting and Gardening during the Eighteenth Century* (2nd edn, Baltimore and London, 1989).
Hunt, John Dixon, *Gardens in the Picturesque: Studies in the History of Landscape Architecture* (Cambridge, MA, 1992).
Hunt, John Dixon, and Willis, Peter (eds), *The Genius of the Place: The English Landscape Garden, 1620–1820* (London, 1975; 2nd edn, Cambridge, MA, 1988).
Jacques, David, *Georgian Gardens* (Portland, OR, and London, 1983).
Mowl, Timothy, *The Historic Gardens of England* (14 vols to date, 2002–).

Quest-Ritson, Charles, *The English Garden: A Social History* (London, 2003).

Richardson, Tim, *The Arcadian Friends: Inventing the English Landscape Garden* (London, 2007).

Sheeler, Jessie, *Little Sparta: The Garden of Ian Hamilton Finlay* (London, 2003).

Strong, Roy, *The Renaissance Garden in England* (London, 1979).

Stroud, Dorothy, *Capability Brown* (London, 1950).

Stroud, Dorothy, *Humphry Repton* (London, 1962).

Tait, Alan, *The Landscape Garden in Scotland, 1735–1835* (Edinburgh, 1980).

Taylor, Patrick, *The Gardens of Britain and Ireland* (new edn, London, 2008).

Thacker, Christopher, *The Genius of Gardening: The History of Gardens in Britain and Ireland* (London, 1994).

Willis, Peter, *Charles Bridgeman and the English Landscape Garden* (2nd edn, Newcastle, 2002).

Chapter 9: America, Africa, and Australia

North America

Fell, Derek, *The Gardens of Frank Lloyd Wright* (London, 2009).

Grese, Robert, *Jens Jensen: Maker of Natural Parks and Gardens* (Baltimore, 1992).

Hall, Lee, *Olmsted's America* (Boston, 1995).

Leighton, A., *American Gardens in the Eighteenth Century: For Use or for Delight* (Boston, 1976).

Otis, Denise, *Grounds for Pleasure: Four Centuries of the American Garden* (New York, 2002).

Ray, Mary Helen, and Nicholls, Robert P., *A Guide to Significant and Historic Gardens of the United States* (Athens, GA, 1982); revised edn published as *The Traveler's Guide to American Gardens* (Chapel Hill, NC, 1988).

Roper, Laura Wood, *F.L.O.: A Biography of Frederick Law Olmsted* (Baltimore, 1973).

Schinz, Marina, and Zuylen, Gabrielle van, *The Gardens of Russell Page* (2nd edn, London, 2008).

Walker, Peter, and Simo, Melanie, *Invisible Gardens: The Search for Modernism in the American Landscape* (Cambridge, MA, 1994).

Central and South America

Eggener, Keith, *Luis Barragán's Gardens of El Pedregal* (New York, 2001).

Eliovson, Sima, *The Gardens of Roberto Burle Marx* (London, 1991).

Sub-Saharan Africa

Fairbridge, Dorothea, *Gardens of South Africa* (London, 1924).

Australia

Aitken, Richard, and Looker, Michael, *The Oxford Companion to Australian Gardens* (Oxford, 2002).

Australian Garden History (journal of the Australian Garden History Society, from 1989).

Dixon, Trisha, and Churchill, Jennie, *The Vision of Edna Walling* (Hawthorn, Victoria, 1998).

Tanner, Howard, *Converting the Wilderness: The Art of Gardening in Colonial Australia* (Sydney, 1979).

Postscript: the future history of the garden

Bormann, F. Herbert, Balmon, Diana, and Geballe, Gordon, *Redesigning the American Lawn: A Search for Environmental Harmony* (New Haven, 2001).

Robbins, Paul, *Lawn People: How Grasses, Weeds, and Chemicals Make Us Who We Are* (Philadelphia, 2007).

Index

Index

Garden History

SOCIAL MEDIA
Very Short Introduction

Join our community
www.oup.com/vsi

- Join us online at the official Very Short Introductions **Facebook** page.
- Access the thoughts and musings of our authors with our online **blog**.
- Sign up for our monthly **e-newsletter** to receive information on all new titles publishing that month.
- Browse the full range of Very Short Introductions online.
- Read **extracts** from the Introductions for free.
- If you are a teacher or lecturer you can order inspection copies quickly and simply via our website.

NDSCAPES AND
EOMORPHOLOGY
Very Short Introduction
Andrew Goudie & Heather Viles

ndscapes are all around us, but most of us know very little about how they have developed, what goes on in them, and how they react to changing climates, tectonics and human activities. Examining what landscape is, and how we use a range of ideas and techniques to study it, Andrew Goudie and Heather Viles demonstrate how geomorphologists have built on classic methods pioneered by some great 19th century scientists to examine our Earth. Using examples from around the world, including New Zealand, the Tibetan Plateau, and the deserts of the Middle East, they examine some of the key controls on landscape today such as tectonics and climate, as well as humans and the living world.

www.oup.com/vsi

SCIENCE FICTION
A Very Short Introduction
David Seed

Science Fiction has proved notoriously difficult to define. It has been explained as a combination of romance, science and prophecy; as a genre based on an imagined alternative to the reader's environment; and as a form of fantastic fiction and historical literature. It has also been argued that science fiction narratives are the most engaged, socially relevant, and responsive to the modern technological environment. This *Very Short Introduction* doesn't offer a history of science fiction, but instead ties examples of science fiction to different historical moments, in order to demonstrate how science fiction has evolved over time.

www.oup.com/vsi

THE MEANING OF LIFE
A Very Short Introduction
Terry Eagleton

'Philosophers have an infuriating habit of analysing questions rather than answering them', writes Terry Eagleton, who, in these pages, asks the most important question any of us ever ask, and attempts to answer it. So what is the meaning of life? In this witty, spirited, and stimulating inquiry, Eagleton shows how centuries of thinkers - from Shakespeare and Schopenhauer to Marx, Sartre and Beckett - have tackled the question. Refusing to settle for the bland and boring, Eagleton reveals with a mixture of humour and intellectual rigour how the question has become particularly problematic in modern times. Instead of addressing it head-on, we take refuge from the feelings of 'meaninglessness' in our lives by filling them with a multitude of different things: from football and sex, to New Age religions and fundamentalism.

'Light hearted but never flippant.'

The Guardian.

www.oup.com/vsi